The Memory Eaters

Elizabeth Kadetsky

THE MEMORY EATERS

UNIVERSITY OF MASSACHUSETTS PRESS • AMHERST & BOSTON

Copyright © 2020 by University of Massachusetts Press

All rights reserved

Printed in the United States of America

ISBN 978-1-62534-502-8 (paper)

Designed by

Set in

Printed and bound by

Cover design by

Cover art: Artist, title, date. Permission credit.

Library of Congress Cataloging-in-Publication Data

<to come>

British Library Cataloguing-in-Publication Data

A catalog record for this book is available from the British Library

This is a work of creative nonfiction. The events are portrayed to the best of the author's memory. While all the stories in this book are true, some names and identifying details have been changed to protect the privacy of the parties involved.

for Alexander

*And so it was that as each tasted of this honey-sweet plant,
the wish to bring news or return grew faint in him: Rather he
preferred to dwell for ever with the Lotos-eating men, feeding
upon Lotos and letting fade from mind all memory of home.
I had to seek them and drag them back on board. They wept:
yet into the ships we brought them perforce and chained them
beneath the thwarts, deep in the well, while I constrained the
rest of my adherents to hurry aboard, lest perhaps more of
them might eat Lotos and lose their longing for home.*
—*The Odyssey of Homer,* translated by T. E. Shaw

Contents

Acknowledgments

This book got its real start in Karen Braziller's workshop at the redolent Winkelman spice loft in Tribeca. I am indebted to Karen for her energy, dedication, perseverance, edits, and vision, as I am to the many brilliant minds who moved through her chimeric meetings with me in the early 2010s. This book was written over the course of fourteen years, during which time I was graced with many crews that sustained me intellectually and took care of my soul: book group, the red car gang, the NER team, "the squad" in State College. I'm also indebted to the English Department and the creative writing program at Penn State, which in 2009 took me in as an emerging writing fellow on the strength of this project and then let me stay. While I fear I may inadvertently leave a name off this list, I extend special thanks to Daphne Beal, Elyssa East, Dana Kinstler, Helen Klein Ross, Oona Patrick, Liz Welch, Meakin

Armstrong, Betsy Carter, Catherine Chung, Alexandra Horowitz, Sally Koslow, Aryn Kyle, Jennifer Vanderbes, Kristen French, Beth Harrison, Robin Beth Schaer, Carolyn Kuebler, Emily Mitchell, J. M. Tyree, Robin Becker, Bill Cobb, Charlotte Holmes, Julia Kasdorf, Shara McCallum, Mark Morrisson, and Toby Thompson. For your edits and comments on early drafts and excerpts, thank you, Michael Archer, Randall Babtkiss, Mira Bartok, Melissa Carroll, Peter Catapano, Nicole Cooley, Michael Dumanis, Bob Fogarty, William Giraldi, Alissa Quart, Kate Taylor, and Josh Weil. At my job, I am lucky to work with a fierce and inspiring cadre of professional women. Hester Blum, Tina Chen, Alison Condie Jaenicke, Cheryl Glenn, Debbie Hawhee, Leisha Jones, Janet Lyon, Carla Mulford, Marcy North, Susan Squier, Lisa Sternlieb: I am grateful for your comradeship and support.

Thanks also to the Parés and the many Franco-American cousins who communicated with me during the twenty years I spent researching the story of my mother's youth, particularly Fleurette, Hank, Madeleine, Marguerite, Regis, and Roger. Special thanks go to my second cousins Jennifer and Stephanie for being there for my mother. To my sister, Jill, thank you for living through it all with me, and for your strength, generosity, and willingness to let me tell my story. Imad joon and Sascha bachcha: mera dil tumse pyar karta hai.

Thanks also to the Kadetsky-Robbins and Kadetsky-Solomon-Barrow clans—Ann, Cathy, David, Greg, Laura, Marilyn, and Peter—for your interest and faith in this project.

I also owe gratitude for the gift of time at several artists' residencies: at the Djerassi Foundation, the Virginia Center for the Creative Arts, VCCA at Le Moulin à Nef, and the Studios at MASS MoCA.

Many of these chapters appeared in earlier versions, as excerpts, or in nascent form in other works. I am grateful to the editors of the following publications: "Ghosts and Chimeras," *New England Review*; "Floor Models," *New England Review Digital*; "Modeling School," *Antioch Review* and *Going Hungry: Writers on Desire, Self-Denial, and Overcoming Anorexia* (Vintage Anchor); "Absences and Outages," *Women's Studies Quarterly*; "Living in the Moment," *New York Times* "Happy Days" blog; "The Memory Pavilion," *Post Road*; "The Oracle," *Mission at Tenth*; "Bombing the Ghost," *Agni*; "Swerve," *Going Om: Real Life Stories on and off the Yoga Mat* (Viva/Cleis Press); "The Wallet Lady," *New England Review Digital*; "Moths," *Guernica*; "The Art of Defying Death," *New York Times* "Happy Days" blog; "Meditations on Survival," *Bennington Review*.

Rebecca Ebstein and Kelly Kanetani provided editorial assistance, while Guy Donahaye, James Huang, Cyndi Lee, Frank Mauro, Joe Miller, and Michael Sonnenschein provided friendship and yoga. Chris Barounis, Alec Julien, and Deborah Solomon were invaluable resources in piecing together my family's past in the New York of the 1970s and 80s. Courtney Andree, Dawn Potter, Rachael DeShano, and the team at the University of Massachusetts Press were beyond professional in looking after every detail and shepherding this book to print. I can't imagine a better home for this book, and for that I owe huge thanks to judge Jeff Parker for honoring it with the first Juniper Prize in Creative Nonfiction.

As Tobias Wolff has written, "this is a book of memory, and memory has its own story to tell. But I have done my best to make it tell a truthful story." While the tale herein is my own, I hope that it resonates as true equally for those who know the principals and for those who do not.

The Memory Eaters

A Taxonomy of the Unknown

Perhaps because so many things disappeared in our family—records, memories, the rings from my mother's two marriages, the wedding silver—my mother undertook many quests for the past. Not her past, or even our family's per se, but past lives, past selves, genealogical doppelgängers. Because of her quests, I know about several of these imagined pasts, which don't quite make up for the evanescence of our tangible one but at least give us a sense of shared history.

For instance: we are said to be descended from Ambroise Paré. My mother—whose mother was a Paré—always said this was more than coincidence. The cousins had us believe that this supposed forebear—"the doctor," they called him—"invented" ether, the gas—or, rather, discovered its usefulness in medical procedures. The family myth is perfectly suited to us, given that ether is more weightless than air: misty, celestial, and smelling of lightheadedness. *There is no coincidence,* my mother said.

It turns out Paré's link to ether is probably not true, though it is true that, before Paré, surgeries were performed without anesthetic. Paré discovered the use of local anesthesia for battlefield wounds, which made possible the discovery three centuries later of ether as a general anesthetic. In any case, it is said that Paré's battlefield innovations transformed medicine and brought it into the modern age. Before Paré, men wounded in battle often died of shock from pain, in part from the cauterizing of lost limbs. Paré also outmoded this practice.

Paré was chief surgeon to four kings in sixteenth-century France as well as to Catherine de Medici. His second "discovery"—hermaphroditism—formed the basis for his opus *On Monsters and Marvels* and earned him the moniker "demonologist." It was published in 1575 and reissued in the nineteenth century—and then by University of Chicago Press in 1982 as a touchstone for sexuality studies. His book is often cited in the same breath as Michel Foucault's *Abnormal.*

I like to believe there are ancestral teachings to be gleaned from our supposed forebear's work on monsters as well as ether. Rather than to hide, or deny, what didn't belong, Paré gave it a place in the taxonomy of the known.

There are several things that cause monsters.
The first is the glory of God.
The second, his wrath.
The third, too great a quantity of seed.
The fourth, too little a quantity.
The fifth, the imagination.

Rationality and the intangible play against each other in this passage, as if Paré can assure us that the uncomfortable or inexplicable is actually acceptable, a thing to observe and deconstruct—which is perhaps my own task.

"Do you know who your daughters are, Michele?" The home care aide, Veta, shows my mother two portraits, of Jill and me. "Do you know their names?"

"No. I don't know. But don't worry." My mother turns to me. She takes my wrist and smiles. "I don't know my name either."

"Really?" I ask her. "What is it?"

"Meephu, something like that. But don't worry, I won't—" She cuts off, searching for the words.

"Forget me?"

"Forget you."

She flits off in a dance, humming and pacing with a red carnation between her teeth. Her lipstick is red to match her scarf, which she draws wide across her arm span. Then she shifts to sashaying, like she used to do when she was a model on the Seventh Avenue runways. She frowns, then brightens, then moves back across the apartment in a dance-like stride. She was never one to dwell on the negative.

Later, out for a stroll by the Long Island City waterfront, we walk arm in arm. The Empire State Building casts a long shadow over Gantry Park. "You're so pretty," my mother says, ignoring my questions, or maybe just hoping they'll dissipate. "I love you. You should be so proud of yourself. Good for you!" she adds, apropos of nothing. "Don't ever get old!" She leads me in a skipping motion, and then, walking, she says, like she always says, "The beauty of the situation is—" she directs me, but with hesitation now, down her block "—everything is always new. Beethoven. It's like I've never heard it before. A bird flying. Everything, it's like seeing it the first time."

And in a crisis, I think, *all you need do is pause, until the knowledge returns, of where you are and why.* That's what she was doing the time she got lost—ten hours after she went out to the store for milk. She was discovered pacing back and forth in front of a guard station at the Queensbridge housing projects, about two miles from home: waiting, waiting until it might come back to her, what she'd gone to the store for, where the store was, where was home. It was 3 A.M.

Ambroise Paré was also a dabbler in alchemy, a more than passing interest for my mother over the course of her life. After she gave up modeling, my mother became a professional astrologer while also holding a day job at the Carl G. Jung Institute in Manhattan. Until about 2005, she co-edited and sometimes wrote for a journal called *Urania: The Journal of the Uranian Society.* One of her publications in the journal was a translation from *L'Astrologie et les Sciences Occultes,* "an examination of early Hermetic works on astrology, magic, and alchemy," according to my mother's preface. Other parts of the original, she wrote, treat "the Corpus Hermeticum, the religious and philosophical documents of Hermeticism."

Hermeticism and the occult suggest a sort of a hiding that was always in character for my mother (*hermetic:* reclusive; *occult:* secret), so I'm surprised when I receive an email seeking further information about her translation. The emailer attaches a PDF of my mother's published piece from the journal, an act that in itself seems to defy the very tradition her translation describes. My mother's now twenty-year-old preface went on to explain that the French text, dated 1942, was a translation from the classic Greek, from a larger work focusing on the historical figure Hermes Trismegistus. "Who was Hermes . . . this mythological figure to whom is attributed the foundation of Western occultism?" my mother asked, as if to suggest things hidden or kept from light. Earlier scholars, she posited, "fastidiously dismissed the body of Hermetic 'magical' texts as unworthy of consideration."

Not so anymore. The emailer is a publisher of esoteric astrology books, and he asks me to pierce my mother's files seeking background on *L'Astrologie et* . . . and hopefully further translations from the French. If I succeed, he will bring forth an edition of the entire project; he will bring it to light (*published:* public).

I agree to help, in part because of what happened over the spring—her getting lost. I've already shifted my mother's files to my apartment across the river in Manhattan to prepare for her inevitable, imminent, move to an assisted living center with full-time care. The files have pointed me to my own quest of sorts, for a past I perhaps somehow missed. She is losing hers, ours; I don't even know if she had hold of it to begin with.

But if a history resides in her documents, so far they reveal a muddle. Their beguiling suggestion is that a past is right here for me, so easy to reconstruct, or that I might, even, locate an origin story for this illness. The very existence of these papers belies their confounding vagueness.

The items fall in no particular order: Jill's and my report cards from when I was in first grade and Jill third; photos; notebooks and bills; pamphlets and mimeographs on esoteric astrology that are not the sought-for French one; charts with makeshift financial planning. Binder notebooks are jammed across the diagonals. Snapshots line the bottoms.

Presences mask absences. My mother was a collector of things that did not require collecting.

I toss into the *discard* pile:

- credit card offers from over a decade ago, one with a Post-it: "New credit cards? Check out."
- notes from conversations with tech support
- used envelopes with information scrawled on the outside about Jill's health
- handwritten tables tracking electrical use in her apartment in Long Island City

Modeling shots turn up, talismans for the quest. I create a makeshift gallery using my bookshelves, floorboards, kitchen counter. The photos are from sixties Boston and seventies and eighties New York. I put one on my desk from the early sixties before Jill and then I came along, and then in the kitchen I place a more candid shot, from the era when our mother worked for Paulene Trigère—a seventies doyenne, my mother's then protector and supporter.

Snap!—my mother is on a runway in a satin-crèpe and velvet evening gown, smooth as champagne. *Snap!*—she is an Eastern princess in lace appliqué bridal gown beneath a wedding cake chandelier and waterfall marble stairway. They are merely records of single moments. Where are the moments in between?

The clutter masks elisions. So much missing. On autopsy, the brain of the Alzheimer's patient can weigh as little as 30 percent that of a healthy brain. The tissue really does grow porous. That brain has been described as looking like a loose, hooked crochet. It is a sieve through which the past slips.

Alzheimer's is about vacancy. But what excuses these files, which ostensibly predate the Alzheimer's?

There is little trace of my father, only hints. A photo of my mother thin and lanky with a big belly rising out of fashionable capri pants reveals a person carefully scissored along the outline of her profile: nose, chin, gigantic belly. She is nose rubbing with that person. It looks like a vase, the empty space where my father should be.

He also exists, through indirection, on a bundle of airmail sleeves addressed to "Mish and Pete" from my mother's then best model friend, Rusty, in 1962 and 1963. There are hundreds of dispatches from Rusty's life in Italy during the early days of Milan mod. Rusty eventually becomes traveling model to Emilio Pucci. She portrays her cohort like artists in ateliers. Fashion ingénues were treated lavishly but earned barely a cent. She was so poor she often couldn't afford a postage stamp. Her employers put her up in the fanciest hotels and delivered gifts of flowers and gorgeous designer dresses and sometimes stalked her and tried to trick her into "Italian marriage," aka sex with no commitment, in spite of her refusals. Her accounts are vivid and alive and lurid with color, thick between the seams. This is a life.

She's also irate, insistent. My mother hasn't been responding to Rusty's letters and cards. My mother has been absent.

Miss you sooo—ache to see you again—Let's hope that it's soon. I love you all sooo . . . still could murder you for

*not writing—what's up—Don't you love me anymore???
. . . Please write. Miss you both like mad.*

*Just returned from Torino fashion show with all Roman
designers—they flipped—I'M IN!! Hope you're both
okay—how about a letter you miserable wretch—Love
you both.*

*Have sent you one letter & 8 post cards and I'm glad I
didn't hold my breath while waiting for an answer. Can't
stay angry at either of you for longer than a second. So
now that I've blasted off—how the hell are you??*

Why was my mother always dropping out?

No one has ever explained to me exactly how Ambroise
Paré is related to us. I suspect my mother never probed the
connection, its apparent rightness having ipso facto proved
its validity for her. This can't explain the ardor of my mother's cousins, who drop references to Ambroise at every
opportunity and in most cases keep *On Monsters* . . . on the
shelf if not the coffee table. It's nice to have a famous ancestor, one who helped along the evolution from dark ages to
enlightenment. As for our family's precise connection to
Ambroise Paré, the cousins say, while squinting: *We are
vaguely related. . . . We have a dim connection. . . .*

My mother's family goes back to the settlers of Québec, this is more clear. The family is, as is said in Québec,
pure laine, 100 percent wool. The line is easily traced on my
mother's maternal and paternal sides. Being pure wool is a
point of pride for many French Canadians, who boast one of
the world's most active genealogical cultures and who con-

stitute one of the earth's most insular genotypes. According to one genetic study, 90 percent of Québecois people can trace genes to the seventeenth-century French founders, a group only about 1,500 strong.

One night, parsing the documents, I discover a family tree in a file of my mother's marked PARÉ. This past clearly once meant a lot to her, though I'm not sure exactly why. She wasn't close to her immediate family, so why such pride of place for her ancestral one? It documents our Paré line going back to the French settlers, originating with one Robert Paré of France. I wonder if this Robert was, like Ambroise, significant to my mother for a reason. But, no, he was not an alchemist but merely a carpenter. Perhaps his usefulness to my mother was only to connect us to Ambroise, so I set about bridging genealogies between the two men. Ambroise was admitted to the Royal College of Surgeons in Paris in 1554. According to my excavations on Geni.com, Robert, my great-grandfather to the ninth power, was married in a chapel in Québec City in 1653, a century after Ambroise's admittance to the college. An obstacle arises: there are five generations missing between Robert's first trace and Ambroise's last.

Ambroise's *On Monsters* . . . so ardently pursues other mysteries that I wonder, fancifully, if perhaps it can illuminate this one. I reach for my mother's copy, extracted from one of the boxes. The cover depicts a one-legged, ostrich-clawed, winged and horned angel-like creature with a third eye in its knee and mermaid-like scales bedecking its torso, a drawing of the sort Ambroise commissioned for his research. "Winged monster," it is labeled.

According to the book's preface, Ambroise fathered nine children, four of whom died as infants. Among five girls and four boys, the fates took all the boys. The longest-surviving son lived nine months. Ambroise had no heirs by the name Paré, in other words. His connection to our family is at best . . . *tenuous*. It is intangible.

Deeper in that same box is a sleeve containing my mother's travel documents from a trip to Mexico with her mother—Grandmaman—in 1984, including my mother's visa, a mimeograph of the travel agent's flight information, and a letter from Grandpapa. On the largesse of Grandpapa, my mother and Grandmaman went to Club Med in Acapulco. "It will keep [your mother's] mind occupied," Grandpapa explained to my mother, about his funding the trip.

Occupied to avoid what? I wonder. *Why this family habit of secrets, denial, sidestepping?*

I do remember the trip. On her return, my mother told a story of going for a walk in the early morning by the violent surf. She tore off her clothes and flung herself in. She was never a strong swimmer. A wave pummeled her to the sand; she couldn't pull herself from the water. She survived. I wonder what trajectory our lives might have taken had she succumbed, as people famously do in the Acapulco swells. Maybe it was around this time I first noticed she seemed absent in other ways. Perhaps she returned from the trip a ghost.

The story of New France is thick with fairies and angels and prophecies—perhaps it's this magical component that made it resonant for my mother. We know from genealogical records that Robert Paré, Grandmaman's great-grandfather to the sixth power, joined a slow trickle of pioneers who followed after Samuel de Champlain, whose first journey to the New World took place in 1603. The record documenting the plight of colonists such as Robert tells of much the same warfare and much the same push and pull as most every New World settlement tale: famine in the homeland (wheat and other grain) set against commodities in the promised one (fish, wood, mines, beaver fur, cattle- and farmland) promoted by royals eager for taxes (the Bourbons: Henry IV, then the Louis's XIII and XIV) and national export operations eager for lucre (Rouen and Saint-Malo). There is an anointed navigator (Champlain), a man with moxie, megalomania, and misfortune enough to instigate several ship voyages and medieval-style warfare with maces and bludgeons to subdue natives (Iroquois Mohawks).

A genealogical website in Montréal devoted to the thousands of Québec Parés describes Robert Paré as "enigmatic." He was one of eleven born to Mathieu Paré in a town in Old France called Saint-Laurent. But because there are several Saint-Laurents in France, no one knows which it is. Several genealogists on the website speculate that Paré's Saint-Laurent is near Orléans. More easily documented is the fact Robert got on a ship and washed up near the rocky breakfront near what is now Québec City sometime around 1650.

The record gives details about another Generation One ancestor of our family, from my grande-grandmaman Léa's paternal line, born in Chambois, Normandy, in 1623. So begin another 1,024 genealogy stories with the same broad outlines. For in a well-preserved settlers' genealogy, if every line is traced the eleven steps to Generation One, the yield for one mixed-breed, twelfth-generation, amateur genealogist such as myself is necessarily 1,024 ancestors. That is simple math.

The purpose of genealogy may be only to flatter one's mortality—or, alternatively, to tell ourselves stories with which to distract ourselves from weightier problems.

My mother saved acres of genealogy files but nothing from her own childhood.

I am fond of this ancestral story for its numinous aspects: François LeRoux—Grande-Grandmaman Léa's great-grandfather to the fifth power—sails into the rocky shoal of Canada's coast one middle of the night in a cool September 1665 as a conscript for King Louis XIV. A salty mist tangles his thick black mane and scrubby sailor's months-at-sea beard. He is feeling a bit ship-sick, but he is bold, trained for combat—and don't forget love—dressed in sweat-acrid, coarse-woven, blue-white sailor's naps. He pukes anyway. There is a lusty future awaiting him on the land side of shore.

The ship is le *Saint-Sébastien*. His regiment is the Carignan-Salières, and he is a member of an esteemed 1,200 dispatched to give backup to the missions, which have been beset by uncooperative natives. François is among 450 from this contingent who will, later, answer a plea from the king to stay on as settlers; that the king promises a transport of French wives makes this attractive.

The purpose of François's regiment was summarized in a letter by the Ursuline nun and mystic Marie de l'Incarnation. "The ships have all arrived, bringing us the rest of the army, along with the most eminent persons whom the king has sent to the aid of the country. They feared they would all perish in the storms they braved on their voyage. . . . [W]e are helping them to understand that this is a holy war, where the only things that matter are the glory of God and the salvation of souls."

It is true the storms nearly spiraled those soldiers to sea bottom. However, certain sailors had a vision on deck:

Sainte Anne came to them. The sailors begged her for help. Shipwreck, otherwise, was certain. The sailors promised to build a chapel in Sainte Anne's honor should she bless their journey and rescue them. She complied.

Magic—the intangible, the evanescent—is in our French Canadian blood. An ocean of documents—birth certificates, marriage licenses, death certificates, liens, citizenship papers—shows, first, where sex was had; next, whence progeny sprang; third, where a grave was dug. But the charts get away from us anyway and transform to snarls, like balled-up yarn undone by a cat. Trace two paternal lines and there is a cogent human tale lurking beneath this timeline, of love and pathos and yearning. Then add one maternal line, then a maternal line for each maternal line. Then cousins marry cousins and nieces uncles. Two brothers Paré marry two sisters Lessard. One of the sisters is Grande-Grandmaman Léa. The other is her sister Aurore. The offspring will be what the family calls "first-first cousins" or "cousins on both sides." Two of the Paré first-first cousins marry men with the last name Roy, so they are Madeleine Paré Roy and Marguerite Paré Roy.

Should genetics have been a field during the times of Ambroise Paré, such prolific intermarriage would surely have interested that distant relation and student of marvels. When I look at the names on the charts, though, aberrance doesn't come to mind for me, in spite of the intermarrying. I imagine each ancestor a perfect child, pink and soft and dewy bright, with the proper number of limbs and fingers and a healthy sheen to the skin. Every time I discover a relation in those archives, I feel a small thrill, a burst of aliveness. Each discovery affirms my vibrant presence in this world. Each name represents a hero. The records are silent about illness and other mishaps of the sort documented by Ambroise, "demonologist."

Our ancestor Marie Renaud was great-grandmother to the great-great-great-grandfather of Marie Jacques, my great-great-grandmother. From Saint-Marceau, Orléans, Marie Renaud was a mail-order bride, though speaking more elegantly she was something called a *fille du roi*—daughter of the king. Louis XIV recruited her and 699 others, women fifteen to thirty years old, future wives-of-someone, someone not yet known to them. Recruit is a euphemistic term for what likely drew Marie, as coercion or desperation or force was probably part of the tale. Marie was an orphan, or a widow, or both, we could say. She sailed nauseous with hunger and longing and regret. I imagine there was a family back in Orléans whom she missed—perhaps a man or boy or girl. She ached for the musty scent of dirt and hearth. In the mist out in the open ocean there rose angels and the Virgin and Sainte Anne, speaking to that ancestor in tongues, words mysterious and gurgling like waves slapping a ship deck, whispering salves and wordlessly humming.

There is a mirror staring us down from the ceiling reflecting on a glass tabletop that is pitched at an angle to reflect both a window and a mirror on the wall, which, in turn, reflect inside each other. We are in a looking-glass tunnel boring through history. We have a high tolerance for confusion in this family, for inaccuracy and forgetting. Maybe this is why, in the files, there is a problem not only of elision but of too much information. We can't keep it all in our heads, so it gets twisted and jumbled and we throw up our hands. *We are vaguely related,* we say. The listener probably has no idea how complicated this really is. We can't say exactly how we are related, because to do so would give us a headache. But we know things are not entirely coincidental, and that everything that happened, it happened for a reason.

I am back in Long Island City with my mother. We have lunch. I ask about the hidden or lost Hermes Trismegistus files. I can't find them. "Yes," my mother says. "I can't exactly recall," she adds, squinting. She doesn't like questions. "I don't know, honey. You talk."

I tell her about the stories I've uncovered from our genealogy, and she nods and says, "Really!" and "Wonderful!" and "You're so good at this!" About the venue, she says, "What a great place. I've lived upstairs all these years and never been."

I say goodbye and get on my bike and pedal fast toward the housing projects where she got lost, then up to the Queensborough Bridge. Up top I can see across the river to Manhattan. Our old home is visible, where I grew up starting at age nine: a white brick high-rise on East Seventy-seventh and the East River called the Pavilion. I remember the night we moved in, and how my mother installed new lamps on the walls with an electric drill. Once the long laborious process was completed, one of the lamps blew. The lamp rained black soot all along the new wall. I offered an illogical interpretation to appease my mother—"Maybe it didn't burn?"

"Of course it's burned! It's soot!" She'd fritzed, just like the electrical cable. She wielded the drill at Jill and me.

"Don't you threaten me," Jill gave back. She walked out the front door and slammed it behind her.

I stormed after Jill but missed her at the elevator, so I went down on my own. I wandered through the new neighborhood and then over to the East River with its effluvium of sewage and everyday discards—a *Mad* magazine, bubblegum wrappers, a cotton ball with Christmas-orange nail polish, wrappers from Stella D'oro and Stouffer's. Walking south along the river drive that night, I'd closed that very same expanse between our building on Seventy-seventh and the bridge on Fifty-ninth where I am riding now—from our history to our future, past selves and past lives colliding with present ones.

As I ride, now, a mist rises off the water and cools my face. I see ghosts of old relations in that brume. I see my mother and Jill and myself, our past selves and our current ones. Each of us is a doppelgänger for an invisible or imagined ancestor, and each forebear is in turn whole and healthy, with ten fingers and ten toes. Ambroise studied aberration. Could he have predicted what would become of our small family, what became of my mother, her lost memory, or the self she maybe left behind in Mexico? How would Ambroise have made sense of this version of her, the woman meandering in the projects? I think of her wandering her neighborhood, drawing routes and then losing them before she can trace them back. Was Ambroise even one of us? Like so much about our family, the answer is ineffable, weightless. We are ether.

Modeling

Tante Annette was a model at Peck's, where there's the L. L. Bean outlet now. "Annette was so tall," Grandmaman used to say.

"*Oo, ooo la la,*" my mother would say. "Tante Annette was my role model," added my mother, who went on to become the floor model at Lord & Taylor, circa 1976. She walked the main floor greeting people and looking tall, in Charles Jourdan shoes.

"Your mother was a floor model at Peck's," Grandmaman said to me, another time.

"Lord & Taylor," I say.

"She was so tall and pretty. *Jolie. Mon dieu,*" Grandmaman said, crying, with tears popping from her eyes, and she drank straight from her bottle. Why was Grandmaman crying? Why did she ever cry? Life, joy, remorse. Her second baby died of a disease—congenital, or environmental, perhaps.

"It's my mother who worked in New York," I said, and she looked at me and said, "You're so pretty." The bottle was Grandmaman's pollution.

Peck's was near the mouth of the Androscoggin, just inland from where the Bates Mill gave its effluent to the river. The Androscoggin, during the mill days, was the most polluted waterway in America. On the town side of the factory, girls called out the windows to the boys from Bates College—which my father would later attend. *"Oooo méchant canard—"* Oh, wicked duck. *"Alouette . . . gentille alouette—"* Oh, pretty lark. They made thick navy-wool blankets. I still have one, with a red and white striped satin border and my name on a white label sewn for summer camp.

After 1917, every mayor in Lewiston was French. Grande-Grandmaman Léa came by Grand Trunk Rail in 1905, a middle child among nine. Féline, her sister, worked in the mills. No one else in the family worked in the mills, said Grandmaman; only they did. The family talks, instead, about the cousin who also became mayor, and how Léa made magnificent hats for Anglos and was tailor to the wealthy of Auburn, across the frothy Androscoggin. She rode in a carriage with her hair piled high and wearing tailored dresses. They talk about Grand-Grandpapa Philippe, who died early, of meningitis or some toxin, possibly alcohol.

My mother talks about how she used to be the floor model at Peck's.

"No, that was Tante Annette," I remind her. "You were the floor model at Lord & Taylor."

"Oh, Annette. I loved Annette. She was so elegant. Who did you say?"

"Annette."

"*Ohhh.*" My mother peers off. "Who's Annette?" She looks round. We're at a family reunion, hosted by Cousin Roger with the Gallic chin and Vichy mustache. Tante Terry is here, and my mother's childhood best friend, Cousine Raimonde, who lived with the family in Lewiston. Tante Simone, Tante Annette, Tante Fleurette: they have all passed on by now, of old age. Oncle Roger: he died jumping from a train near a lumber farm outside Montréal. Oncle Raymond, who never got over World War II: they say alcohol took him as well.

My mother takes my hand. She never drank, never worked in the mill. What was her toxin? "Who are all these people?" she asks me. "They keep hugging me and asking how I am." She is very slim and her hair is dark and dramatic, and she is beautiful, so people hug her.

"They're your cousins. Remember Raimonde? You called her Taffy."

"Taffy," my mother says. The past is there before her, across a spray of water. "*Taffy!*"

Ghosts

The landscape is pragmatic and stretched out, with mini-malls dotting the roadside. I'm seventy minutes into the forty-five-minute drive, lost, just like when I was a kid. This crossing, from Newton to Boston's northern suburbs, always defied one relative or another. I wonder if my mother felt this same claustrophobia before she fled to New York. She escaped, and only rarely looked back. "It doesn't need a sign, everyone knows it's 128," my father always says.

I take a breath, sip from my water bottle, turn into a gas station for directions. It is 1997, and I am on a journey of return to the place my mother escaped from—or was exiled from and lost. I have received a grant from my graduate school to pursue this research, but so far, aside from and probably including my mostly dishonest grant application,

I have failed make its aim clear to others. My project, to inhabit my mother's past in order to resolve something that I don't even know what it is, has left me disoriented and aimless in my travels.

I do know what I am looking for. Only, it's hard to ask about it. No one wants to talk. "Nobody ever talked about it," a cousin of my mother's told me as I prepared for the trip. "They hid those things." Another said, "I don't like to talk about it because it's not nice."

"It" is Renée, or, the world that came to be in the orbit of Renée's illness. Why pretend I didn't come here with the preconceived notion that my mother's faraway stare, her lapses, her silences, her outages, owed, somehow, to the situation surrounding her younger sister? Why am I, too, a conspirator in this silence?

I already know the skeletal frame of this story that seems shaped by absence—an X-ray story. My mother was two and a half when Renée was born, a "beautiful child" who never learned to talk or walk, and had a gate on her bedroom door to protect her from . . . *what?*

I have tangible memories of Renée, though of course I never knew her. She was a ghostly presence in the household where I grew up. When I turned eleven, Renée's age at death, I often stood in front of the bathroom mirror mouthing on loop, *My aunt died when she was eleven years old. My aunt died when she was eleven years old.*

My attention wanders back to the car. I'm having trouble staying in the present moment. The past keeps superimposing itself—even my body feels like my younger self's. I finally locate Grandmaman's house, a stone Tudor with fairytale red trim around the door; it looks virtually unchanged. I slide my vehicle to the curb and suddenly I am eleven and Grandmaman is leading me from the doorway back to the curb, where her olive-green Mustang awaits us. I get in, noticing how Grandmaman's hands are addled by a tremens from the night before. I feel the weight of the car door as I close it. I hear its slam. My lap belt attaches with a click. I feel the numb premonition this car ride will kill me. As it turns out it doesn't, but certainly something was lost.

In 1997 I have been taking a graduate course about transgenerational trauma—"the phantom." This concerns "memories of loss in the second generation," as Katherine Hodgkin and Susannah Radstone later describe it. *Post-memory* is another term for this quality specific to traumatic memories that morph across generations, transmuting and taking residence in the consciousness of the young. The memories are "dispersed," "transmitted." Children of trauma survivors, write Hodgkin and Radstone, are "haunted by memories which are not quite their own." Over time, such memories take on new shapes; there is, write the authors, "a sense of sliding, elusive truths, which change shape and meaning as decades advance, as children take up and share and examine and revisit parental memories."

"Escape," write Radstone and Hodgkins, "may not be all it seems, and the children will carry that past forward into the future."

I return to the present. Grandmaman pulls open the door and stands behind the screen. Her hair is white and shimmers so that she looks, actually, like a phantom, and she is stooped to an almost ninety-degree angle. I have forgotten her eagle nose and luminous, olive-brown skin. It's been more than ten years since I've seen her. She is now eighty-four or eighty-five, depending. Uncle Phil has told my mother, who has told me, that Grandmaman recently broke her hip and is housebound. She doesn't know that liquor stores deliver, but that hasn't made her less delirious. She has dementia, as *if* she's still drinking, Phil told my mother. Perhaps it's what they used to call wet brain. Grandmaman's whimsical grin is the same.

"It's Lizzy," I say.

There is recognition. "My God, I wouldn't know you! So you're Lizzy?" I notice with an odd feeling that she has an accent, twangy and French Canadian, that I never noticed before.

We sit inside, on the same old couches, over the same unvacuumed Oriental carpet. Clutter used to stay contained in her art room. Now, envelopes line the walls of the living room in tall stacks—entry forms and award gifts from Publishers Clearinghouse contests, including several cheap necklaces and earrings in plastic jewelry boxes. There are also buttons, and beads ordered by color and size into Lucite cases. We used to string those beads onto long acetate threads to help create an ever-thickening bead curtain separating the dining room and kitchen. The curtain, I see now, is extant. When I was a kid there were the happy times—nighttimes—and the uncomfortable, cold, sickly ones—daytimes. Now, though it's daytime, there is the joy of nighttime. Grandmaman winks at me and smiles and pinches me. "My God, you're Lizzy! I love you!"

And because this is the fun, nighttime Grandmaman, I hug her. Since I have ostensibly come to see her as part of my research, I ask her questions, about everything except what I need to know. I ask about her relations in Maine, aware that's not really what I'm after. I ask about French

Canadian food and culture. I tell Grandmaman I remember her listening to Édith Piaf. I remember her singing along: *Je ne regrette rien,* pronounced French Canadian—*regrett-tah.* I don't regret a thing. Then she'd rattle off to us in French in an attempt to teach us phrases: *C'est si bon! Mon dieu!*

"Piaf!" Grandmaman grins that capricious, conspiratorial smile. "I love Piaf. You know there is some Piaf, over there. Under the shelves." She gestures, coaxing me, but because I don't see a phonograph, or the old LPs, and because I have mixed feelings about becoming her co-conspirator again, I stay seated.

Grandmaman has moved on. "Oh, pretty goose," she's saying. She is evoking her home town of Lewiston, Maine, when she was a girl. "The girls used to call to the boys from the top floors of the mill." She imitates their coquettish French. *"Gentille ah-louette.* We used to get jealous. How can you call from the windows?" She talks about when my mother was a model at Peck's Department Store, even though that was Grandmaman's sister Annette. "Michele is five foot nine," says Grandmaman, though my mother is five foot ten (or eleven, depending). "And she went with a football player with blond curly hair at Bates"—meaning, again, Annette. Then Grandmaman complains that Annette converted to Judaism, though in this case that was my mother.

Apparently past and present are as superimposed for Grandmaman as they are for me—this presence of ghosts, this overlay of past on present. What is it, this habit of memories from previous generations taking over the stories of those still living?

Now she tells me about how she came from Canada, though I know she didn't. That was *her* mother, Léa. "Oh,

Canad-aaaa," Grandmaman is saying, wistfully, French-style, though I'm pretty sure she's never been.

Grandmaman and I hug again. This gives me an odd sensation, as if by embracing her I can get something back, or walk through history and start again, relive it better this time. Mine is not the life I was supposed to have.

In 1997, my half-sister, Laura, is at Yale. I went to a state school, and there is student debt. In New York, my full sister, Jill, has been through detox from heroin three times in the last year. I anticipate the loss of Jill, or I am grieving the old Jill before she quit her job and the workforce and became someone else. My father and stepmother, who have not seen Jill since Laura's bat mitzvah nearly a decade ago, have taken to pretending Jill doesn't exist—erasing her.

How far into the past would I have to go anyway to remake myself, to recast fate? How many generations into the past must I traverse to create a world in which Grandmaman wasn't an alcoholic, my mother not numbed to Grandmaman's psychic violence? How many steps back makes my father behave better in the divorce, makes him stand by his children, say aloud to the world that we are not dark baggage from a broken past.

Eleven. I still have a pearl necklace de-acquisitioned to me that year by my paternal grandmother—Grandma Bea—with eleven pearls. It's an add-a-pearl necklace, the style where a necklace with one pearl is made for a girl at age one, and the family adds a pearl every year. Only, after I turned eleven, no one was going to add more pearls, so Grandma Bea gave it to me. I still wear this incomplete necklace, seeing it as a sign of how my father's family forgot me after the new child arrived. Wearing this necklace makes me feel sad, and yet also defiant. *I refuse to be invisible,* is what I mean to say to the world by wearing it.

Also when I was eleven, my father and stepmother gave away my name. In the Jewish tradition, a child cannot take the name of someone still living. Something about stealing that person's soul. My baby half-sister, Laura, was given the middle name Beth. I'm sure it was unconscious, my father and stepmother's desire to make me a problem that would disappear.

During the course of my research trip, I look up Renée's birth, death, and institutionalization records and interview numberless cousins. I aim to resurrect eleven-year-old Renée, to blare out the fact of her existence into the abyss of silence and hiding.

In the surviving pictures she is about age four, doll-like in a frilly, white, communion-style dress. With her porcelain skin, big black eyes, dark hair, and red lips, she is the picture of tragedy. In one photo, Grandpapa's legs appear behind her and his hands support her by her arms. In others, she lies on the ground and holds herself up by the elbows. "She'd just fall," says my mother's cousin Regis. "She had the smile of an angel."

Aside from epilepsy, her illness is never named. "No one ever said what was wrong with her. She fell off a bed and hurt her head, I think," says Regis. The records also offer no clue. There is a record of a visit to a neurologist at Boston Children's Hospital at age eight. Soon after, Renée was moved to a state hospital for the epileptic in western Massachusetts, presumably on the advice of the neurologist. After the move, the family drove from outside Boston to the hospital, in Palmer, every two weeks. Once, Renée had a chipped tooth, likely from a seizure. She died at the institution, during a seizure. "Asphyxiation due to Epileptic Seizure. Status Epilepticus," reads the death certificate, meaning, according to Google, a seizure that was persistent or repeating, lasting at least five minutes.

I understand that stigma would have affected other families in this situation, too. According to lore, the institution—Massachusetts Hospital for Epileptics, or, later, Monson State Hospital—was in the nineteenth century a fabled repository for the indigent, the outcast, the mentally ill, and epileptics. Through the 1930s, rumors circulated that it housed a eugenicist and mistreated its charges, resulting in a history of questionable deaths. Siddhartha Mukherjee's *The Gene* discusses the role of such institutions in efforts at genetic cleansing starting in the late 1900s—stockpiling epileptics, poor people, the promiscuous, and sufferers of mental illness. The larger gene pool would benefit from the ostracization of these subjects—their early deaths and failures to reproduce, went the thinking. In many cases, they were sterilized.

In my family, there was certainly silence. According to my father, my mother never spoke of Renée.

"Your mother's sister died of infantile syndrome," Grandma Bea says.

"But she died when she was eleven. And what's infantile syndrome?"

"I have no idea. It's what the family said."

"She died of epilepsy. She was mentally disabled."

"I didn't know that. Well, that was not something they would have shared with us."

It is easier to discover the effects of Renée's illness. According to her relatives, Grandmaman was "broken" by the illness and death. After the funeral, Grandmaman sat out on the porch drinking straight from a bottle and wailing, "My baby! My baby's died!" No one appreciated Grandmaman embarrassing them like that. "Drunk, for all the town to see," says a cousin. "Practically on the street like that, howling into the night and cradling a bottle."

Say what you will, but I see Grandmaman refusing to carry forward the silence and erasure. Grandmaman blared out the fact of Renée. Renée existed. Renée was real.

I can't speak so directly with Grandmaman, but I begin to feel emboldened about bringing up Renée with people more removed from me, as if I am merely a journalist investigating the family secret of a distant clan. I call one of Grandmaman's cousins saying I want to talk about Renée. She invites me to meet with her and two of her siblings in the parish office of the Catholic church where one of the three, Father Paul, is the priest.

It's a hot day when we meet, and the rich, velvety curtains are drawn. There is a lush red carpet and ornate, soft furniture, which all give the spacious, high-ceilinged room the feel of a regal court. It is as if we are all assembled here to absolve Grandmaman, or, at least, understand better the circumstances under which she created misery for others.

Still, we deflect. The siblings are warm and jovial. Perhaps because I've never met them before, they want to, first, aid me in grasping the intricacies of the family history. One of the cousins, Marguerite, is a historian of Franco-American culture, and all three are concerned, if not amused, by the lack of knowledge in the general population about the prolific but small French community that settled in New England in the late 1800s and maintained its insularity and tradition against many odds. The three cousins often break into French, a twangy and nasal vestige of what is spoken in Montréal.

Though I have asked about Renée, and they have acknowledged her, they want to first help me understand one origin story for our immigrant clan that particularly reveals the French Canadian diaspora. This involves the double marriage of the two sisters, Léa and Aurore Lessard, and the two brothers, Philippe and Cyril Paré. The first marriage took place in Beauce, Québec, where the family fled from cold and famine in 1905 to work in the wood and paper mills in nearby Maine. The second marriage took place in Maine. So the siblings' mother is Aurore, who was the sister of Grandmaman's mother, Léa, while the cousins' father, Cyril, was the brother of Grandmaman's father, Philippe. There were sixteen children of this double marriage, including Grandmaman and the three siblings. To make things more confusing, there seems to be, among this French Canadian tribe, a shortage of first names (not to mention last). Also, it was common in my great-grandmother Léa's generation for the mothers to bear as many as fifteen children, to lose at least three in childbirth or infancy, and to lose several adult children along the way. The lines are hard to distinguish, and the many cousins hard to tell apart.

I notice a funny quirk: the cousins keep getting me mixed up with my mother. Marguerite refers to me as "Renée's sister," "Solange's [Grandmaman's] daughter," even "Michele." For Paul and Madeleine, I am Grandmaman's daughter, Grande-Grandmaman Léa's granddaughter. No matter how many times I correct them, I get a dim, squinty, putting-of-things-into-place. "So, your grandmother . . . ?" Renée is always going to be my sister. Grandmaman, with her lunacy and alcoholism, my mother.

This all gives me a weird sensation—shortness of breath, a feeling of suffocation. The cousins' confusion is understandable given such a large family. With so much hardship and so many crossovers in its history, it's not so surprising that people—and some facts—fall through the cracks.

But the story of names also seems to describe an ethos in which no one owns their own individuality. Unlike the Jews, the French Canadians have no superstition associated with name sharing—my first cousin, Nicole Langelier, has the name I always choose in pseudonym games: my middle name plus my mother's maiden name. The Jewish censure against double naming is linked to the Hebrew language's habit of placing importance on the name, and on the word. The word for God cannot even be spoken, and is referenced in the Hebrew texts by other codes such as the anagram YHVH. Your name is not just a stand in for your self. It *is* your self.

Among French Canadian Catholics, your name is your mother, your aunt, your cousins. It connects you to your community. All of this makes me want to escape, just like my mother did. But if I did so, I, too, would be complicit in my own erasure.

I track down more cousins. The story of Renée is forever displaced. One effective subject changer is our illustrious (and false) status as descendants of the famed and celebrated fifteenth-century French surgeon Ambroise Paré. Another is the truer story of our patrimony in the town of Beauce, Québec, home of the miracle-inducing Sainte-Anne-de-Beaupré chapel and a landing site for the seventeenth-century French settlers of the Americas.

A less flattering but omnipresent replacement story is that of the family's alcoholism and addiction. Grandmaman inherited her alcoholism. Grandmaman's drinking got bad after Renée's death. Or, it was Renée's illness that drove Grandmaman to drinking. Above all, genetics drove Grandmaman to drink.

Grandmaman's uncle "L'Noir" died falling off a train from Canada to Maine coming back from a lumber camp in Gault, outside Montréal. They found him dead in the thawing snow the next spring. "He had problems. The same problem," says a cousin.

Grandmaman's mother, Léa, would go fetch her husband Philippe out of the bars. Philippe died at age forty, in 1923. People blamed a bad liver, though the death certificate names a two-month bout from "multiple neuritis," or meningitis. "Drinking problem," says another cousin.

I wonder, though, if my family's propensity to addiction is less easily explained by a simple gene like BRCA-1 and more akin to generational trauma, epigenetic tendencies.

Epigenetics is the recent science describing the hereditary qualities that accrue when a gene or chromosome is triggered to its active state. If your mother gets breast implants you are still likely to have small breasts, or if your father walks with one foot pointed outward for life because of childhood polio you will still walk straight. Nonetheless, there is the possibility that you will inherit certain "marked genes" for less tangible traits acquired during an ancestor's lifetime, such as trauma. In a sense, epigenetics is the science behind the metaphorical notion that we carry the psychic wounds of our parents and parents' parents and parents' parents' parents.

In 1997, pre-Google, my immediate Jewish relatives were spared the knowledge that a branch of the Kadetsky family did not get out alive. But for the American Jew, has anyone ever needed particulars for the death camps to seem a personal, ancestral tragedy? My great-great-grandfather Abraham Kadetsky immigrated to New York City from a small town northwest of Warsaw in 1879. At thirty-one, I didn't yet know that others stayed behind and perished at Auschwitz. And yet there is that kind of anxiety an acupuncturist will point out to you, that she feels it in your pulse. It is the pulse of war survivors. Or it is tachycardia. I always knew I had it.

The epigenetics of trauma is often conflated with Jewish experience. Second-generation descendants of Holocaust survivors are often associated with transgenerational PTSD, or, colloquially, "Post Holocaust Stress Disorder." But I wonder about the ripple effects of a trauma, global or personal, in any person's life. For how many generations does it persist, and, perhaps more relevantly, how does one end the cycle and inoculate one's offspring?

Why did my Jewish family erase me, erase Jill? Did a capacity to forget bring my parents together, and bind their two families in a pact of mutual denial and negation? Or is it simply that given the choice between a straightforward and happy narrative and a more complicated and dark one, every family will choose the sunnier one? Then, inevitably, the person who acts out the unhappy subplot is tossed aside.

Epigenetics was discovered thanks to, in part, a multigenerational study on survivors of the so-called tulip famine in 1944 in Holland. People ate tulip bulbs to survive. Those who did survive—Audrey Hepburn was one—suffered chronic problems with blood sugar regulation for ever after, as did babies who'd gestated during that period. Starvation, it seems, forever disrupts a body's ability to process glucose. But oddly, the same effect was found in offspring of the survivors, and those offspring's offspring. While once genes seemed to be destiny, in this case it appeared that genes were switched on by environmental causes and passed down to future generations in the altered form.

The mnemonic of the tulip helped me grasp this elusive concept when I read about it in Mukherjee's book. At about that time I disinterred approximately 2,000 daylily bulbs—relatives of the tulip—from an enclosed garden bed in my backyard in Pennsylvania. I learned that daylilies are considered an invasive species, and invade they had done. Underground, I discovered, bulbs in the shape of small, seaweed-like pods were branching out to form rhizomic clusters. The lilies' substrata had imploded. Because there was not enough room in the concrete bed to contain these ever-multiplying bulbs, they had packed themselves in so tightly that they had become a solid brick of the rhizomic pods, with barely any soil between. I tossed the clusters into an ever-enlarging pile. I put the bulbs on the curb, and soon someone, finding them to be pretty, adopted this epidemic-expanding pestilence. When the bulbs disappeared, I felt a weight lift from me. Beforehand, my skin itched and I felt infected. If only I could so easily leave my family legacy on the curb to be taken on by scavengers. But perhaps the disappearance of the lilies freed me in some way.

This primal trauma: my father erased Jill and me when our half-sister arrived. His marriage to my mother had combusted long before, I know this. But why such a price to pay, and why to be paid by me?

I have an image, one that seems to be my own, but perhaps it came from my mother. My father sits on the floor in boxers with a deck of cards, playing solitaire—Scorpion. The transcript of the divorce hearings confirms the image. "He would sit and completely immerse himself in television, newspapers, sit and play Solitaire for three or four hours in a row and just grunt when I would ask him something," my mother testified. I was three at the time of the testimony.

It is only when I study the transcript more carefully, and ask for corroboration from other relations, that I can read between the lines. The story of an affair by my mother is told in the record as a kind of reverse etching. It is told in the omission provided by my father's silence. Like so much about my family, the transcript fails to communicate directly.

My father does not testify but responds in just the affirmative or the negative to each of the six "complaints." Complaints 1 through 3, 5, and 6 are boilerplate, such as our address and the ages and names of Jill and me. It is number 4 that one must read, and reread: "That the Plaintiff has at all times conducted herself as a good, true and faithful wife towards the Defendant and that notwithstanding such conduct on her part, the parties are now living separate and apart." My father contests just this.

I do math. I recall Scrabble score cards in a box belonging to my ex-stepfather that I uncovered during my mother's marriage to him—Mish and Pete on one side, Bob and Maureen on the other. The scorecards had given me a kind of parallax. I couldn't conjure a world in which my father and stepfather co-existed. But, plainly, they all knew each other. The story of my mother's affair with Bob McKee takes form. Of course I'd missed it on first read. In the transcript of the divorce hearing, it was told as an omission, occupying the negative space of the narrative. The scorecard in the box of Scrabble—that, too, provided hints in the form of an erasure. It was as if I'd been reading one of those blackout poems, where lines from a page are crossed off in marker so as to leave only words that cryptically tell a different, often related, story. Actually, it was like reading a FOIA document censored by the FBI.

"The words which the phantom uses to carry out its return (and which the child sensed in the parent) do not refer to a source of speech in the parent," writes Nicolas Abraham in his essay "Notes on the Phantom: A Complement to Freud's Metapsychology." "Instead, they point to a gap, that is, to the unspeakable."

That the affair was never again discussed did not lessen its ripple effect. I never knew about my mother's affair with Bob McKee, but, unspoken, it remained vaguely evident to me. I failed to grasp its exact contour or shape. Secrets are like this. They don't disappear; they just become shadowy and cast an ambiguous darkness.

One example—after I turned fifteen and people started to say I looked like my mother, my father gazed at me as if possessed by a vision and then snapped, yelling for thirty minutes about my carelessness. I'd broken a jar of mayonnaise: that was the presumed cause.

Stories of my ancestral past are crawling into the light, bursting with joy at the freedom. Next I receive a phone call from Regis. He is the son of Annette—Grandmaman's beloved sister. During that summer of 1997, we'd spent a pleasant afternoon sitting at a glass-topped lawn table under the gables beside his pool. His fuzzy cat alternated sedately between his lap and mine. Regis had carted out boxes of family photos and given me several, and then even given me some items from a closet belonging to his deceased wife. He'd hugged me firmly when I left.

"There's something I meant to tell you," Regis begins, slowly, on the telephone now. "I was thinking about it, after we talked. My mother told me Michele pushed the baby off the bed. Maybe Michele was jealous, or angry, I don't know. Maybe they were just horsing around. That's what Annette said. Your mother pushed the baby off the bed. That's what caused Renée's illness."

Regis gets silent. So do I. I have to sit with the news for a long time for it to take full form, for it to make sense, for it to frame the story of my mother's family for me such that, suddenly, everything looks different.

Regis had tried to tell me this already. *Renée fell off a bed and hurt her head, I think.* Michele caused Renée's illness, was what he was trying to say, but I didn't hear it because, somehow, I am still not good at listening for things that have been silenced.

Of course there's more between the lines too. There is a tightly held secret, little spoken, that no one—or not Regis, anyway—has bothered to interrogate. A two- or three-year-old, left alone with a baby, is blamed for a fall or even maliciously provokes it, and thus also causes the illness that will break Grandmaman and destroy their family.

It was all Michele's fault, then: Grandmaman's violent drinking, her passive-aggressive manipulation, the endangering of the grandchildren in Grandmaman's Mustang, her shaky hands. It was *Michele's* fault, and everything that went wrong after, too: Michele's bad marriages, Jill's addiction. And what about everything that went wrong before? Oncle Ray's mania after World War II and his subsequent alcoholism-related death that left poor Taffy an orphan. Oncle Robert's alcoholism. Grand-Grandpapa Philippe's alcoholism. The rampant alcoholism in the subsequent generation. A pattern emerges. No wonder Michele escaped, scapegoated for generations of bad choices or even, if one accepts the theory, bad genes.

Gabriele Schwab, who is German, illustrates the concept of the phantom by describing the idyllic town where she grew up in the aftermath of World War II. She describes "the discovery of a book about the history of Jews in Tiengen, the town where I grew up as a child." She writes, "I felt a shock of recognition when I discovered, like in an archaeological excavation of a city's buried history, the erased traces of Jewish life in my hometown. This is when I realized that, despite my many attempts to learn more about the Holocaust than the sparse knowledge offered to us at school, I had never thought for a moment that the persecution and deportation of Jews during the Nazi era could have included the small medieval town where I grew up. My own unwitting complicity in not asking about the history that was right there in front of me is a typical unconscious mechanism of children born after violent histories. Silencing the past by not wanting to see is one of many such futile attempts to numb the inheritance of pain, guilt, and shame of the second generation."

It was right in front of her. This revelation seems to bind together the stories of second-generation inheritors of trauma. We knew it all along, but because it was never spoken, we never fully processed it. In the very same gesture, we were handed both the information and the mechanism by which to pretend it didn't exist.

In his 1998 essay "Buried Homeland," Aharon Appelfeld writes about his return to the small village in the Carpathian Mountains where he spent his childhood. Here, his mother was among sixty-two mostly women and children slaughtered by the Nazis in 1941. On Appelfeld's return in 1995, he spends several days searching for the mass grave where his mother was buried, but the townsfolk stolidly deny its existence. Finally he discovers its whereabouts. "It turned out that what the people of the village had tried to conceal from me was well known, even to the children. I asked several little children, who were standing near the fence and looking at us, where the Jews' graves were. Right away, they raised their hands and pointed."

Later in the essay, Appelfeld describes the environs as "full of ghosts."

Secrets, silences, ghosts, incomplete scenarios from which we build our own identities. How to heal from such incompletely told traumas? "What I call 'haunting legacies,'" writes Schwab, "are things hard to recount or even remember, the results of violence that holds an unrelenting grip on memory but is deemed unspeakable."

In another narrative, perhaps Renée is born with fetal alcohol syndrome. But no one ever talked about the silent narrative, the damning one, so no one ever cleared Michele of her unspoken crime. Silence, and not alcohol, is the real killer here.

"What happens when we build a grave within ourselves?" asks Schwab. "While we can foreclose mourning by burying the dead in our psyche, those dead will return as ghosts."

Writes Paul Celan: "No one / bears witness for the / witness."{Might need to be cut/altered for permissions purposes.}

In August of my research summer, my mother offers to meet me for a side trip to Maine. I arrange a rental car, and watch as she emerges from the bus and strides into South Station in Boston. She greets me warmly, looks around with a single sweep of the head, and says curtly, "Let's get out of here, fast." I drive us to Old Orchard Beach in Maine, a destination for the Québecois where she—and her mother before her—enjoyed summers during her childhood. We spend the weekend at a bed and breakfast, where the restaurateur treats us to his slurs against the "French" and we pretend we aren't "French." We eat at lobster shacks and explore the nearby beaches by car.

I ask her about Renée, and about the affair.

She gets a refracted expression, pleads ignorance, acts confused. I show her the pictures from Regis. It's all far in the past for her—a past studiously, deliberately, actively forgotten. Over the course of the trip, she never admits to me she'd been scapegoated for Renée's illness, and by extension for everything that went wrong after (and before). I begin to suspect my mother never admitted it even to herself, or even spoke of it. Her studied avoidance about the affair with Bob McKee is perhaps, more so, evasiveness.

From there, I travel on alone to genealogical archives in Québec, and then return for my final year of graduate school.

I wish I'd asked Grandmaman about Renée. I wish I'd pressed my mother about the rumor. I wish I'd pushed through her coyness about her affair.

Marianne Hirsch coined the term *post-memory* in the essay "We Would Not Have Come without You." It describes a trip during the 1990s with her parents to the city of Czernowitz—in present-day Romania, where Appelfeld noted the presence of "ghosts"—in which her parents seek to show her their memories of 1939, when the Nazis imprisoned them in the city's Jewish ghetto, stripped them of citizenship, and caused them to ultimately flee Europe (and survive the Holocaust). Hirsch deems the trip a success because she, as the child of Holocaust survivors, is able to put a picture to stories told by her parents that have shaped her consciousness since childhood. For her parents it is a success because they are able to integrate their happy memories of the place from before the Holocaust with their traumatic ones from during, and contextualize those with the present-day city and their present-day lives.

Perhaps I have accomplished closure for myself in making this return, on my own, and then with my mother to the place of her birth. It is very different from Hirsch's trip to Czernowitz, but, then, the ghosts of my ancestors weren't banished from this place. Perhaps they still hover.

Or perhaps I do not find closure until I dig up those rhizomic lilies in my backyard, those many years later. Or never. But I must.

As I write this, my father, now eighty-three, is hospitalized for the third time in as many years for small illnesses that become large at this age. Does death free us from anger? Jill has been hospitalized as many times in just one year, because of accidents that occurred while she was buying drugs or after. Was her terrible chronic malady fated by genes, by the circumstances of her (our) primal trauma, by the synergistic charge set off by the coupling of two parents who were traumatized by their various histories?

It's six and a half years since my mother passed away. She died on the winter solstice. Because she'd been a professional astrologer, an astrologer friend of hers interpreted the astrological chart for her time of death. That astrologer said my mother "couldn't have chosen a more propitious time to leave the earth." The stars were aligned, said the astrologer, to release a cycle of ill will back out into the universe. "Her death ends the cycle." It was an astonishing statement, since the astrologer knew nothing about the particular details of the unfair, unspeakable burden of blame carried around by my mother for her entire life.

Perhaps because of the echo to my would-be aunt's death at that age, I've always felt that a piece of me died when I was eleven. The car ride with Grandmaman, the necklace, the theft of my name—circumstances aligned at that time to rob me of so many things aside from and including my innocence. In an epigenetic scheme, every event echoes, and like a sound wave intrudes upon the silence of the future and resounds ever forward to not-yet-experienced other futures. But I wonder about turning the echo backwards onto the past, remaking that past using the wisdom of the present. Can the present echo backwards, thus silencing the reverberations of these undying traumas? Perhaps I *can* get something back—walk through history and start again, relive my life better this time. To do so I fear I must forgive the slights of my past, if only to free my future of the past's echo. Metaphysically, that might be hard. But it is my aim. Epigenetics, taken metaphorically, teaches us important lessons about fate. Fate, actually, is not fate. I am drawn to this promise of freedom.

Absences and Outages

We took trips as a family to the Jewish stalls on Orchard Street, to hunt for new fashions. Our mother had regular work on Seventh Avenue runways now, but she'd been shut out from photography. "You're gorgeous, but you're too old," a top agent for print had told her. She was thirty-five. We'd only just arrived in New York, and already her time was running short. On Orchard Street my mother imagined new careers for herself.

We walked to Orchard from the subway at Bleecker and fell into the bustle of black and white all-of-a-kind family members. I recognized these people from books, in the All-of-a Kind-Family series, about an Orthodox Jewish family on Delancey Street. I felt sorry for the girls and women of this family who had to wear dowdy matching black jumpers while their cluttered stalls held the handbags and belts that were the ingredients of "new looks" for us—we outsiders traveling to them from alternate realms. Our immersion in the project of style felt out of tune with the shtetl atmosphere.

I remember my mother picking through plastic packages at a table with a sign reading $1 APIECE, and how I felt an oddness before a gray-bearded shopkeeper with a yarmulke who watched us from the other side of the table, Holocaust numbers on his forearm. The shopkeeper seemed to know what we were looking for, perhaps knew all about our plight as outsiders and about shape shifting and the power of surfaces and the skill behind the craft of assimilating; how succeeding could be a matter of sliding through cracks, of becoming silent and invisible. He glanced at the clothing as if he understood already what we wanted to be wearing that season, as if, sagely, he knew exactly the right tension we must establish between extraordinary beauty and fitting in.

"I can buy clothes in men's shops!" my mother might have exclaimed just then, a common refrain of hers. I might have looked back at her from this paradoxical moment and noticed her thick, cascading hair and her cheekbones and her beauty even without makeup or jewelry. "Who knew?" she might have been saying, as went her chorus. "All my life I've been trying to fit inside clothes that are too short in the torso and too wide in the ass. Why can't people just do what they want?"

Trauma and celebration intertwined. An interplay of darkness and hilarity created a lack of reality. A traumatic filter descended between oneself and the world. One disconnected and acted strange, sane in an insane world. A glance was shifted politely away, the tattoos never discussed; there was no way to make sense of the irrationality.

In an unliteral way, perhaps I understood that the tattoos spoke to a personal kind of horror too. The Kadetskys had left the Old World in the 1870s, and Jill's and my Jewish relatives didn't speak of the Holocaust. It was too grand and big for talk, it seemed—a large blank spot scissored from a photo. An absence. That I was Jewish felt visceral but also vague to me. It was only that summer that I even got my name back—Kadetsky—as I'd endured the prior three years under my stepfather's patronym, McKee. We'd fled his home in Westport, Connecticut, that spring, and when we arrived in New York at the start of summer, Jill brought me to register for fifth grade the following fall at P.S. 158 on York Avenue. We'd entered at the broad steps of the school's double doors and walked up a wide staircase with sculpted banisters. At the second floor the grandeur gave way to industrial urban, with pale aquamarine wall paint and a clerk's window with a metal grille in front, as if to protect the clerk from the likes of us. She handed me a form and told us to fill it out; Jill grabbed it from me, and I looked over as she penned in precise capitals, letter by letter, my new old last name: KADETSKY.

On the way back inside our building I felt strangely changed by this new revision to my identity, emboldened by a mix of exposure and, if unrealistically, also anonymity, as if my new-old name were actually a pseudonym, myself an imposter posing as . . . myself, a new-old version of me. Who *was* I, anyway?

I'd often felt I was hiding, or living a secret life. For instance, I had memories from our time in Westport that I knew were possibly not real. I believed I should keep them to myself. They had a quality like the memories of dreams, and I didn't know if in fact I'd actually dreamt them.

In one, I was on the path to my elementary school there. This was a shortcut that began in Bob McKee's backyard and involved climbing over several low walls in the town's ancient interworking of granite rock barriers, each separating one property from the next. The last crossing deposited the walker at a bluff above the athletic fields at Hillspoint Elementary School—"the whale," people called the building, because of a bulbous slate roof that resembled a sperm whale cresting above the surface of the ocean.

Jill and I usually walked this route together, but she often was sick with allergies or bronchitis or the flu and stayed home. I also had friends at the end of our long driveway and sometimes met up with them, but there were plenty of times I was on my own. In my memory I crossed over a low stone wall from one backyard into the next—I didn't know the residents. It was fall, and the yard was covered with dead leaves that made a crunching sound. I trod carefully, walking toward a patio made of slate pavers. There were pieces of lawn furniture and items such as ashtrays and matches and cups; the ashtrays had spent butts, and the pillows on the furniture lay awry in their cases. It was as if the family had only recently gotten up. On the other end of the patio was a sliding glass door cracked open just an inch.

I walked to it, touched my fingers inside the gap, slid open the door. I slid it shut the same degree, and then walked inside to a modern kitchen, with tile and a Formica island. There was no sound but the refrigerator and a breeze from outside. I walked on tiptoe around the island to the refrigerator, and I opened it. There were leftovers, some milk, butter. I quietly closed the refrigerator door, and then retraced my steps and exited carefully so as to leave the slider in its original position.

I continued on my way to school. Or perhaps I was coming home from school and returned in the direction of our backyard with its climbing tree, its eighteenth-century well, our mother's flower garden with its snapdragons and dahlias.

Even since coming to New York, I had dreams about the transgression—the yard, the slider, the cool feel of the countertop on my hand. In the dreams I was sometimes with someone else, a boy. Was I remembering a dream, or an act? Maybe I'd done this with a boy? Maybe it never happened?

Something about this man holding the dollar-apiece socks, his unwavering stare with its cool remove and insistence, made me feel seen, my foibles revealed. I could no longer take shelter under the cover of invisibility. I was a Kadetsky again. Had my father even noticed? I was invisible in Boston, and no less visible before the men in public who stared and leered. They couldn't see me, couldn't get inside me because I knew how to disappear for them. When I was invisible it was as if I didn't exist or, rather, that I existed but in a liminal other world, like the dream state where I'd penetrated—or not penetrated—the neighbor's slider in Westport. I'd had another invisible, secret place in Westport too: an imagined room, off to the side of my bed, where I connoitered with the kidnapped Patty Hearst and dressed in princess costumes with the celebrity captive, my make-believe friend.

My mother kept the name from her defunct second marriage. I think she did it because *McKee* was neutral, a name that could fit anything inside of it. As a McKee, she could walk through the world a WASP.

Our building was a city of false identities. The door across from the mail chute belonged to a childless, middle-aged couple who hollered at each other night and day, first the woman, then the man. Now, voices spoke in sharp whispers from behind the door. I wondered if they were whispering because they knew I was there. We often heard them from inside our apartment—through our metal door, all the way across the hallway, and through their metal door. Sometimes the couple got silent, which turned out to be even more frightening than their shrill, soul-piercing wailing. "Bloody murder," my mother would say, or, "She's blistering him like hot water." Then there would be a looming silence. My mother would purse her lips and stare at our door. "She killed him."

Now the man's voice was saying again and again, "I'm leaving. I'm leaving now." I considered whether he meant permanently or just at the moment, which was what I hoped, because I'd never seen him in person. The woman had turned up at the elevator once. She wore a dusty yellow wig and looked faded all over, in a conservative skirt suit with a long blazer in a dull brown with big buttons. She'd nodded to me in a quiet, docile manner, and I'd thought it was funny I'd never have known about her New York accent if I hadn't heard her spitting blood at her husband and scorching him with her words.

I waited at the elevator without pressing the button, hoping the man would turn up. In the silent hallway, the elevators dopplered when they flew up and down past our floor.

I heard several while I waited. Finally the lock tumbled in the couple's door, and as the man approached through the hall, still out of sight, I pressed the button. Perhaps he'd heard me leave the apartment those several minutes earlier and knew I'd been there. I felt suddenly exposed, but when he arrived I could tell he barely noticed me.

He matched his wife exactly, with dusty brown hair and a clean-shaven face and a broken, sad manner. All the way down in the elevator, he didn't look at me at all. Utter strangers might appear at your elevator bank, it was true—I was always appearing at the elevator banks of strangers. But I knew him, I knew his secrets.

I wondered what other unresolved pasts he might remember, and why he put up with the screaming. His papery hair made me think of him as a ghost, wandering in our hallway. Maybe his diaphanous self came into our apartment from time to time and mingled with our other ghosts, like the couple in the shop downstairs where I bought my mother cigarettes: the woman with the orange hair who looked at me through her glasses skeptically, cocking her head slightly. "For your mother, dear?" *For yoahh mothah, deaahhh?* I'd nod yes, and then notice, as she flipped over the pack to check the price, Holocaust numbers on her forearm, a pale blue like her veins.

The Holocaust couple in the store downstairs were papery like the couple across from us too. Maybe they were ghosts, too, or had died in the Holocaust and become new selves.

I go over these memories trying to figure out if my mother deliberately made herself absent as well, or if, rather, her relentless optimism was in fact real. I think of her on seedy and smelly Houston as we made our way to the clothing stalls. There was music in the air. The O'Jays' "Love Train" might have blared from a boom box, and there would have been garbage bags piled high still because of the famous garbage strike of 1975. She might have fallen into step behind the man with the boom box and shifted her gait to the rhythm of his music, and then grabbed my hand so I had to change mine to keep step with her. Her hips might have swayed as she strutted with her shoulders and legs and sang along in a whisper, *"People of the world, cha-chaaa. Start a love train, a love train—"*{~?~TN: PAGE \# "'Page: '#'" Might need to be cut/altered for permissions purposes.}

I knew these moves too, from *Soul Train,* but how was one to inhabit the same persona on the street that she practiced while no one else was home in the safe and private interior of her empty apartment? Didn't my mother also intuit the presence of the war's haunting past here? She was born in 1940, a child of World War II. My aunt—my father's sister, born in 1934—still had memories of the war. The wrist numbers told me horror was near, as memory or possibility. Did my mother not feel this as well?

The freedom brought by fashion interacted with a sense of history bearing down here. In our giddiness we discovered our new looks and new selves against a backdrop of other people's traumas. In the distance between the two lay friction, an impossibility of things lining up. And so we disconnected and floated up above and watched ourselves being watched from the safe distance of an unnamed place out there.

My mother was absent, I do know this. There were outages, moments like a radio suddenly bereft of its signal. Jill did a not-so-nice imitation. You'd ask our mother a question, and she'd peer at you with her black imperious eyes. She'd stare for five seconds, ten seconds, maybe a minute. Thinking. Or maybe forgetting, you never knew which, until she would finally answer, but with an answer often unsatisfying. "Well, what do *you* think?"

Perhaps it was only a trick of fate that these often occurred when the topic was fashion. To be a fashion model was to be a scrim. Society projected its vision of itself upon you; you became a thing external, possibly unreal.

My mother's and my shared hobby of watching started then. We watched turns of light at sunset and the way reflections danced along the east-west channels of the cross streets and changes on the urban streetscape subtle or imposing, such as the new kind of Chinese up on First called Szechuan or a boutique, say, where everything— *everything!*—was ugly.

We watched people. My mother was fascinated by the commonplace that what you saw in *Vogue* happened first on the streets of New York. An African wrap headscarf in 1975 on a thin, tall, elegant, black lady dressed up at a disco became a part of the runway chic of seventy-six. There was a democracy to the fashion of the street, and my mother loved this as well. If it looked good, it grabbed someone's eye and caught on. The irony was that it was often the wearer who looked good, not necessarily her costume. No matter. Such was the power of perception. To understand this subjectivity was to understand a gain to be made in manipulating it. I think this notion of an equality of style seemed to both excite and further her idea of herself as a rebel, someone without roots who'd fled several oppressive pasts—as a Catholic, as a housewife, as a young woman at the close of the fifties who for reasons unclear to us sought a break from her New England family.

We also practiced the skill of "noticing." A man's high-water pants made him look shorter than he was; a woman with a bad fit in the underarms had "baggy bosom." First, you noticed whether someone looked good or not; then, you scrutinized that person until you understood why. Young girls in tube tops were all limb and abdomen, their uncovered shoulders accentuating the length of their arms, wrists, fingers, the high cuts of their shirt bottoms creating a false waist and the impression of long, long legs. A big ring on an elegant woman accentuated the grace of a hand.

Her lapses often fell during such moments. "*In*-teresting," she might whisper, and this could be a cue telling Jill or me one was coming on. "I have a theory," she might say, and then she would pause a long time.

Learning style was a matter of getting in tune with that intuitive and visual part of your brain that picked up on things in a glancing kind of way. Later I understood this to explain the outages and their connection to watching, and this turned them into less of a horror. You had to catch your instant's thought—that something looked good—before you applied your brain to the matter of deconstructing why. Only after you glimpsed that nonverbal insight did you then analyze, break down, come up with a plan to re-create. One's own "look" arose from enacting this alchemy. It took several seconds to catch a glimpse of the thing.

These outages also often fell during or after a question had been asked of our mother. We'd look up at her in expectation. "What?" Jill might say, or she might repeat the question.

Our mother would continue to peer off, to a faraway and indistinct vanishing point.

To repeat the question a second time was to invite her ire. Her gaze might snap down at the questioner. "I'm *thinking!*" Often an answer eventually did materialize, and then sometimes it didn't. Often the encounter ended with Jill stomping away insisting our mother was mad at her for no good reason.

I remember less the topics than the settings. One is on Orchard Street while we are shopping or noticing, and there is a theory being formed in my mother's head about, perhaps, the rise of the sexualized male in fashion ads, but more specifically I am aware of the stink of the street mixing with the scent of my mother's perfume—a distinct orange water and clove—and the smell of polyester rising from fabrics in the stalls. I know I feel nervous. These were invisible moments, when seconds seemed to stop moving and all one could do was delay all bodily function until a little bit later, when it was time to catch up with the clock again.

"*This,*" our mother might finally say, spaceship landing. She might point to one of the ads, white-glued to a poster board tacked to the red-brick facade of a tenement behind a stall. "*See?*" she might add.

Of course, we hadn't.

Then she would offer one of her lessons on style.

It was often hard to decide, was she leaving us during those moments, or was she, truly, intuitive?

Beauty was innately wrapped up in disappearing. It was both a reason to disappear and the very quality of disappearance itself. We perfected the art of being looked at while at the same time feeling menaced by the ever-present eyes of the city on us everywhere. Silence and invisibility, like our home at the river edge of the city, were still our safe zones. Inhabiting beauty out in public, we disconnected from ourselves.

Perhaps my mother believed the contradictions would resolve themselves naturally. Beauty was her career, her way of moving through the world. It was Jill who had the luxury of pointing out the hypocrisy. Sometimes she criticized our mother for being vain or "acting like a queen."

"If I am a queen, you are a princess," my mother would respond. I was her more natural ally: I wanted to be like her—leggy, gorgeous, and charming in the lens of any camera. Brooke Shields was an omnipresent vision in our neighborhood, and this affected me too. As the Calvin Klein model, she appeared on subway ads and kiosks and on the sides of buses screaming by—*Nothing comes between me and my Calvins.* And we saw her on the street and in shops because she lived nearby. Shields was a year older than I, and thin and pale and dark haired, also like me. Sometimes I fantasized that she and I occupied the same New York City universe, one whose essential ingredients were models, taxicabs, and glamour.

My mother's work in the field taught me that fashion made constructions of people. She and her best friend from modeling, Rusty, designed several elegant escapes for once they'd aged out as models, each a business plan resting on this notion of building oneself from nothing. It was the last, Body Lab, that ultimately entombed their friendship—a startup in the second story of a building around the corner from Bonwit Teller, Saks Fifth Avenue, and Henri Bendel. My mother and Rusty employed working models who, dressed in lab coats, ushered patients into treatment rooms where medical personnel placed electrodes on the patients' bodies.

This was an ostensible weight loss tool, though it was later proven to have no effect. Still, the high-tech beauty institute may, at that moment, have been ahead of its time.

Modeling school capitalized on the same yearning as the subway and park bench ads: BARBAZON—THREE MONTHS TO BEAUTY AND A NEW CAREER. My mother and Rusty believed they could do a modeling institute better. They were the real thing, after all: towering beauties, barely a half pound each, and graduates of the John Robert Powers School of Charm in Boston. Rusty ran the classes out of her apartment for several months; then a better idea overtook it and it got shut down.

I attended the school's maiden trial, along with Jill and the daughter of a friend of Rusty's. By chance, it provided me with important skills for negotiating life in the city. The sessions taught me to wrap myself in a veneer that could make me impervious to the antagonists. Poise was a buffer—a stance that said to the world, *I am not afraid of you, you cannot touch me.*

Our first session covered the model's walk. This required, first, adjusting our posture. "Lift your carriage and imagine a plumb line pulling up the crown of your head and extending the distance from your head to your tailbone. Tailbone moves in, shoulders travel back and down."

Rusty lined us up at her window wall and pointed us toward her front door. She faced us and demonstrated the posture, first lifting her shoulders in an exaggerated gesture. "Shoulders back," she said—she puffed out her chest—"and down"—her shoulders lowered several inches. Then she turned her back to us and sashayed along the living room floor so that her torso registered hardly any movement other than a gentle, pleasurable swaying and her legs kicked out from her hips in apparent isolation from all other body movement. Then she repeated the walk with a phone book on her head. "Fix your vision on a single point slightly above parallel—the clock," she said as she demonstrated again.

Next it was our turn, a spectacle that Rusty endured for only seconds before demonstrating it to us again.

"Okay," she said after. She directed us back to our starting point. "Shoulders," she repeated, "back, and down."

We rolled our shoulders around.

She looked at us blankly. "Again. Back. And down." She spent the next several minutes reviewing the shoulder roll with us and then ended the session by making us promise to practice the walk for ten minutes every day, concentrating on the plumb line and the shoulders—"Back. And down." Next she'd teach us the turn, in which one foot did not cross over the other.

My training here did not last long, but I did imbibe such tricks of the trade as that runway pivot; the skipped meal; the single-sweet-a-day rule; the shoulders rule; the plumb-line rule; the runway sashay; the gaze; the mechanics of holding one's center of gravity very high up in the rib cage.

It was about this time that my mother began commenting, "You have a protective force around you." I think her impression owed to my newfound confidence on the street. I was smart and adult-like and mystically protected by the universe, she said. I could ride the bus alone and nothing would harm me. Like so much that came from her mouth, these statements were likely one part truth, one part folly, and one part unwillingness to see the world as it actually was.

Jill was less dutiful than I about the project of beauty. She arrived at the modeling sessions a skeptic; it was often painful to watch Rusty through Jill's eyes, to witness Rusty deliver her many bon mots about beauty, often in French. *"Ma chérie. La beauté,"* Rusty might say, *"ce ne pas superficielle—c'est profonde."* I remember she had match-books that read BEAUTIFUL YOUNG PEOPLE ARE ACCIDENTS OF NATURE. BEAUTIFUL OLD PEOPLE ARE WORKS OF ART.

"As my great hero and likeness Catherine Deneuve says, 'The real star of the fashion picture is the wearer—*toi!*" she would also say.

"Deneuve's a blonde," Jill might have pointed out.

"Oh, darling, a joke." She sucked in through her cigarette. "Fashion is optional," she added, "but style is not." She took another drag and made eye contact with each of us and then stood and posed before us with her cigarette before she then paced along the wooden planks of the floor, her gaze directed at that far-off vanishing point.

I would look over at Jill and read in her expression a new pantomime taking form. Jill's irony was a force causing me to feel myself both present and not present, participant and critic.

Our family nevertheless came together over conversations about style. A typical setting was one of the floor mattresses in Jill's and my bedroom, our mother's favorite red crystal ashtray, a pack of Winston Longs, and matches laid out on the ground. Our mother would wear her slim men's blue jeans, belted near the hip, a man's white undershirt, and a pair of Geoffrey Beene tennis shoes—she'd acquired matching pairs for each of us on a modeling shoot. This was her "new uniform," she might explain with great serious-ness. Then she'd instruct us in her philosophy of developing a "look" for oneself—something simple and chic and stun-ning and easily replicated for any day's wear, such as the jeans and T-shirt and no jewelry.

I see Jill mixing us each a cup of powdered café au lait from a General Foods tin, and myself lighting our mother a cigarette and noticing how it gave her fingers an appearance of exaggerated elegance. She inhaled and held her breath before blowing out through pursed lips, then, swirled her powdered coffee to a foam. An empty Entenmann's box and a bag of Stella D'oro anisette toast spilled crumbs onto the top of our bureau. It was well past dark, the dinner hour having come and gone.

We often discussed the business of fashion. Rusty had spoken of perilous developments—assaults on svelte elegance. Our mother, on the other hand, embraced the new trends. The papers were celebrating a movement toward "anti-fashion"—Yves Saint Laurent had called for "the end of haute couture." This style promoted not just blue jeans but also makeup that was specially manufactured to create the illusion that one wore no makeup at all—the "natural look," also called the "no-makeup look." The irony was lost on us, I think, that in our world even a lack of a mask was a mask itself. Working along the same paradox, the *New York Times* fashion supplement had recently experimented by using models from real life.

I remember my mother enthusing about this in particular: "Real people, not models, imagine that." And she would stare off, lost there.

I was hearing a lot now that I was beautiful. Often this was spoken in code, that code being "You look like your mother." I met this as congratulation, felicitation, a charge of relief, expectation, duty, giddiness, promise, and also misgiving. Also, I didn't believe it. My fifth- and sixth-grade school photos showed me a wan, olive-skinned girl with limp straight hair. I was the skinniest girl in my class at the public school, sallow and undernourished, my skin a green-white shade of pale. I looked anemic, likely was.

The street told me I was beautiful. It communicated this through the eyes of leerers that felt like wet hands on me. Greasy bulbous sticky glances everywhere, a city of thick gelatin air grabbing with its invisible reach on us. A stare has no physical weight, takes up no physical space, but has personality, can accompany an onerous implicit manipulation, can say that you, being leered at, are complicit in this act by me, leerer. You, subject of leer, carry a shame greater than mine, leerer's.

It would happen on the bus across town to Rusty's. A man stared. He wore a business suit, carried the *Times*. Beyond this drooler, there was another man staring. Beyond him, who knew how many more—men in wedding rings, men in side curls, men in cassocks, it didn't seem to matter. I tried not look back, with contrived fascination studied the bus ads and their promises for better lives. Learn to be this and learn to be that: *a secretary! an English speaker! Learn the hustle. Go to technical college. Go to business school. Study sewing. Become a fashion designer. Be a model, or just look like one! Lose weight. Gain muscle. Join the Marines.* I was also familiar with the counsel of our exemplary citizens: Mayor Koch says, *Tell your sister to take a bath in a half a tub of water.* Brooke Shields says, *I don't care who wears the pants in the family, just so long as I wear the Calvins.*

The groper, the protector, the lurker, the drooler—the stares wormed inside me and took form in a palpable and almost physical anger.

Beauty could also cause one to believe that she was at the center of the universe, and this, too, caused a dislocation—a feeling of existing five or seven feet above the sidewalk and looking down at oneself as she is being looked at. One's own reflection talks back from everywhere—in the glassy eyes of those lust-drunk men glowering, drooling, pursuing everywhere, and in the window of a subway car when the train pulls out of a station and the darkness of the tunnel makes itself a black backing to the glass, sharp as a mirror now.

On the subway ride home from Orchard Street this trick of the light might happen, and I would watch the three of us lined up like perfume bottles, my mother in the middle, tallest and with the longest torso, then Jill to her right, I to her left, we three repeating images with our long dark hair and thick dark eyebrows each in a different size, and then as in a hall of mirrors we could also see ourselves shining back at us in the eyes of the men, and then we became more dim when we entered the next station, and the tick-tick-ticking of the passing pillars made us look like images in a flip-card movie camera.

Our mother played along when Jill enacted impressions of the lurkers and leerers, but her exact position about the glowering men was unconvincing. She liked attention. One time she had a friend over when I came home from the bus and complained—Niger.

"Mmmhmmm," he said sagely.

My mother made a frown. "Honey, they can't help it." She rubbed me on the shoulder as if I'd won something. "They want to look at you. You're beautiful."

"They like what they're seeing!" Niger agreed.

My mother lived in the world believing—*knowing*—that the eyes of the world's body were on her always. She seemed to regard the appreciation of any reveler as a beam of protection. If the droolers and leerers menaced us, they also had this Janus-like counterpart who admired and protected. Were these two men different? It was difficult to know whether to embrace or reject these men.

I attended an outdoor concert with my mother and Niger once. My mother found a rhythm and danced under the incandescence of the music and lost herself in an otherworldly trance. When the music stopped, she looked at Niger and me and said with breathy excitement, "They were playing for me."

Afterward, Niger introduced us to the musicians. One of them took my mother's hand gently in his and kissed the back of it. "You are a goddess," he said. "I saw you dancing. I was watching you. I was playing just for you."

"*Thank you!*" she responded. I knew that she was thanking him, also, for the favor of shining his music on her and charming her with a spell that had turned her into a blessed, magical being. This interaction was about powers, beauty being only an aspect of those.

I believed I had access to these kinds of powers myself and understood them as linked to that ambivalent haze of attention. I often felt this when I was waiting for the bus. Every time, the driver slid up to the curb so that the door opened directly to me. Every time. When I stepped on, the driver winked and gave me a look—not a threatening one— and then said, *Gotcha!* or *Have a nice ride, sweetie!* I knew he was sidling up that bus just for me, that I was the passenger whose face he most wanted to greet him when he levered open that door onto the smelly and harsh world outside.

The bus's reliable yet magic-seeming slide to the curb a half inch from the tips of my shoes gave me a mystical feeling of control. As it sidled near, I imagined that I was willing the bus to stop right in front of me, and then it did, exactly there, as if it were an extension of my own body. To feel this was to experience myself in a subtle corpus different from my actual one.

Sometimes when I think about them now I feel I somehow understand my mother's outages and performances because I, too, felt I wasn't there. At the same time I was also, like her, perhaps, very present, differently there— often somewhere else.

The Memory Pavilion

In the dream, I am showing off the walls of my new apartment in Manhattan. *See here, the shine?* I point out to my friend. *Here. Look. The texture.* I stroke the new finish to indicate it is soothing to the touch. And to the eyes. The colors are brilliant, luminous—dusty rose in the living room, a pale blue in the bedroom. The painting has come out so well there is a powdery effect, the walls giving a little beneath the gentle pressure of a finger, and they are slightly iridescent. Actually, they are like velvet, with minerals flecked into the weave. Perhaps they are velvet. The blue is especially beautiful, with golden highlights, a quality of goldenness that calls to my mind something I have read about in the Upanishads: *akasha,* the quality of radiance. *Brilliant as 100,000 suns.* This characterizes a sublime state, *amanaska,* a stage of enlightenment in which the seeker transcends the mind, I read.

This is in fact my old apartment, where I grew up, but in the dream I have gotten the lease back, so it's also my new apartment. Unlike all my other dreams in which I move back here, this time neither Jill nor our mother is living with me. This, I realize in the dream, represents a breakthrough.

My subconscious must be getting closer to where it needs to be, I confide to the dream-friend, closer to reconciling its longing for the past, closer to accepting the reality that Jill's and my childhood in which we lived in this apartment with our mother has gone the way memory should go. The past is over. The central conflict of my life, about my yearning for the world of my youth, went and resolved itself. *Once you get your childhood back, there's no more hankering for it,* I say to the friend. *Nope.* Its cathartic nature explains the vision-like, synesthetic, and intensely sensory texture of this particular dream.

My friend is Julian, the child of a psychiatrist, which perhaps explains why he is peering at me with a sage expression, a little skeptically.

More nights than not, I dream about the apartment, given up by our mother owing to unpaid back rent—an insurmountable sum—in 1995. It's our lease that got away; every New Yorker has one. Our old rotary telephone—ringing with calls from creditors—got disconnected, though the number remains framed in my memory, is my password for things lately, and is a number I recite in my head sometimes to hold back nerves.

212–861- . . . , 212–861- . . . . It's an incantation, though whether to bring back the past or make it go away, I'm not always sure.

When I wake up, I have a headache. It is several seconds before I realize that, no, actually, I don't live alone in our old apartment, painted in iridescent blues and golds that evoke a feeling of enlightenment. And also—in spite of my optimism in the dream—no, I haven't yet sorted out this most intransigent conflict in my life, this drive to reclaim my past, or re-experience it, or release myself from the grip of it, or collect it in pieces so I can give it back as a coherent narrative to my mother, who has misplaced her version of it.

My dreams stubbornly encourage me. There will be no relief until they come around: *The lease is gone, get over it!* There's no getting it back.

I feel a pang. My headache reminds me that Jill has been talking about hiding the Advil owing to our mother's taking too much, complaining of headaches. Could our mother's persistent headaches suggest there is a problem larger than Advil abuse, I wonder, still more awake now. Did Jill ever take care of a tooth abscess that was pointed out to us by a dentist six weeks ago? Could the untreated abscess be causing the headaches? Since I woke up, I have had a dull pain behind my sternum. I feel a heaviness. Emptiness. Blankness. Every time I come back from this dream, I have to grieve that apartment all over again. Then those sensations ebb. And now I feel panic.

I call Jill and get her voicemail. At a certain point, maybe in my twenties, I started to feel I was the adult of our threesome. I put that *New Yorker* cartoon on my fridge: *Why do I have to be the only sane one in my family?*

I call my mother, get her voicemail, and then call our mother's adult daycare center to see if I can find her. I get Tamara, a nurse.

"This is serious problem," says Tamara, who is Russian. "I did not know your mother has tooth abscess. This must be taken care of."

"That's why I'm calling."

"Why this not taken care of already?"

"I don't know. The issue is, I'm trying to find my mother to ask about her headaches, if they're maybe actually a toothache."

"Headache," says Tamara thoughtfully. "The other day your mother says she has headache. For headache we elevate legs and give water first. No aspirin. At first, no aspirin. Later, if water and leg elevation not work, we give the aspirin."

I wonder to myself why Russians seem to always drop articles where they are needed and add them where they are not needed. How could not understanding the article rule create such a regular misuse of it? There must be some algorithm.

"I give her the water and then rest and I ask her, how she is feeling?" Tamara says. "'Goooood,' your mother says. So your mother is all right. No headache now."

I imagine my mother lying beneath the healing gaze of Tamara, basking in her care and attention, and then indulging Tamara with a positive report in exchange for her empathic service. "*Gooood.*"

"Tooth abscess," Tamara is saying, "this can spread to brain and cause sepsis in brain. This is serious problem. You must take care of right away." I know, I want to tell Tamara, but the abscess got intercepted. I was looking over there. There was a swerve. Perhaps this looking in the wrong place is what the yogis call *viparyaya*—error—I continue thinking, as Tamara goes on.

Headache, headache. I further tune out Tamara. Her words come through the receiver as a torrent of blurred speech. Occasionally the term *headache* stands out to me, crashing through the monologue like a car careering past a divider line. It awkwardly rights itself after each swerve, and then I hear the torrent of blur again.

What is it exactly, this susceptibility, even desire, to believe that the problem in front of one's face deserves the most attention when it does not, and actually there is a more glaring problem, seemingly hidden, but obvious, maybe like *adrista*—the unseen? Could there be a coherent process at work here, in which the *adrista*—that hidden thing—slowly finds its place in a rational story line, perhaps even the way the dream state—*nidra*—collects fragments of things and arranges them in a narrative? *Blue paint, the apartment, Julian.*

Why we never took care of the tooth abscess, I should be explaining to Tamara, is because I lost track of it. There was a different swerve, to some other problem: the Medicaid application; locating the right day center; finding cash to pay the lawyer; negotiating with Jill about her caretaking, her free rent, her small salary. There was the fact that our mother is dying bit by bit, one brain cell at a time. I allowed my mind to go elsewhere. *Tamara,* I think of confessing to her, *I even liked it, my mind in that other place.*

My mother's condition began to worry me around the fall of 2007. She was just sixty-seven. I wasn't really on speaking terms with Jill. She'd moved into our mother's then-new place in Long Island City in 1997, and things never seemed to get stable for Jill after that.

Now, Jill was calling me to vent. She claimed our mother

was leaving pots boiling on the stove long after there was liquid left to cook them in, and doing things, of an unspecified nature, to endanger the life of Jill's cat, Lucky. "She's trying to kill Lucky," Jill fumed. Or "She's trying to set the apartment on fire." One day, Jill cried into the phone, "You have no idea what's going on over here! You don't understand. Nobody understands."

I did understand, though owing to different signals. My mother had confided to me that she was on probation at her job at the C. G. Jung Institute in Manhattan. While my mother and I were taking a walk together around that time, she also told me she was having strange perceptions, a kind of aura materializing around her and then a sensation of "floating." Around then she and I traveled to Massachusetts to see her brother and his family. Phil had moved into Grandmaman's house after she died in 2005, but it was as if my mother didn't recognize it. One night, she woke up when I came into our bedroom—Grandpapa's old room. Popping up to sitting, she stared at me angrily. "Who are you!?" she accused me, and then looked around the unfamiliar room and exploded, "Where am I?" I noticed that she had covered her bed with items she'd found in my suitcase: my bra, my travel pillow. Then she put her head down on her pillow and conked right back out.

Walking into town the next day, she asked me where we were. I teased her for asking me the same questions over and over.

"Don't do that!" she protested. She stared at me with a particular combination of vulnerability, humiliation, and anger that I hadn't remembered seeing in her in quite that way, and I regretted my words.

One day during that trip, I took out some yarn that I'd discovered in a shopping bag left behind among my grandmother's effects, thinking I'd practice knitting with it. I asked my mother to provide stationary arms to stretch apart a skein while I unspooled it and rewound it into a ball. I'd made a misstep, another of many. She immediately lost track of this task, and quickly got the skein tangled. We set about trying to untangle it, and I watched my mother get lost in each tangle, retangling and folding the yarn and then following its path to its next tangle, until she got distracted and folded that one over and created a new tangle.

That was when I knew this was an illness she had. I didn't know yet, hadn't done the reading yet, that one of the main known characteristics of Alzheimer's is a thread that builds up in the nerve cells of the brain and curves into knots, called neurofibrillary tangles. Seeing my mother tangled there in that yarn, and watching her weave through crowds at the Amtrak station on our way up there, I got my first intimations that whatever this illness, it had something to do with tangling.

"Your mother is so kind, so nice. We enjoy very much working with her." Tamara has changed the subject. She is saying this for no apparent reason except perhaps to acknowledge that our mother, the day center's newest participant, is a welcome addition. But my mother's pleasantness in particular is just a fact of existence that Tamara feels the need to exclaim upon, thus giving us further opportunity to follow a rabbit warren of thoughts elsewhere, away from what none of us prefers to think about, this rot-eating-ahole-in-our-mother's-head problem, this tooth and brain-sepsis problem and neglecting of the obvious.

Everybody loves our mother.

They used to love our mother as well, but Jill and I always felt she was fooling people when we were kids, with that charm of hers, so put on, with that big wide smile that would eat you up. "Isn't it ironic," Jill likes to say now, "that I am taking care of her, feeding her, ministering to her every need, when she couldn't bother to make a meal for us when we were growing up?" It's true, what Jill says. We survived according to our mother's fashion-model diet: coffee, an Entenmann's doughnut or two a day, more coffee, perhaps a small plate of noodles and butter for dinner. One day when I was eleven, my mother told me she'd had a vision that I'd been her teacher in a past life. Shortly after, she said to me, "You don't want to be a kid anymore, do you? That's a box. You don't want to be in that box. I think of you as an adult. Wouldn't you rather be an adult?" I remember it as consensual, this turning of tables. It is, indeed, ironic, I assure Jill, that our mother resisted the role of caretaker.

Jill says our mother is faking it to everyone, even to me, to everyone except Jill, who bears the brunt of our mother's sour moods. Faking it means putting on a brave face, or covering for lapses, such as when someone says to our mother, *It was so nice to see you yesterday*, and she responds without missing a beat, *Yes, it was lovely*.

This, too, sounds accurate. Recently, I saw this faking of things when I brought my mother to an assessment interview for an insurance-covered home-care aide.

"Can you make yourself a tuna sandwich?" asked the intake nurse.

"Of course I can do *that!*" my mother replied with indignation.

The nurse noted this down. I corrected her. The service denial arrived in the mail the following week.

I called in, dumbstruck, and the same nurse confided to me, "You should tell your mother to tone it down a little. Just looking at your poised, elegant mom, someone might say that she doesn't need the service."

In her more authentic state, our mother gets mean and morose and depressed when she and Jill come home from appointments, says Jill, and she cries a lot, and sometimes she moans. "It's the moaning I can't stand." Our mother moans when she's hungry, says Jill, or wants attention, or feels an inarticulate desire for something she doesn't know anymore what it is.

We held our lease in Manhattan for twenty years exactly. It is the first ten of those I want back. In my mind they form an epoch, less a span of time than a block. The heft of that block matches the nostalgia I feel for it, something weighty and substantial, enough so it drives me through the city's streets seeking out my past in that uncorruptedly corrupt state only a New Yorker could miss: the new Bendel's, laid out like the old; the new MoMA, so pointedly evoking the last.

Our era begins in 1975. Our mother was newly divorced for the second time, newly escaped from yet another claustrophobic suburban marriage, eager to find her way again as a model in the world of high-glam fashion. She was thirty-five years old, five foot ten (or eleven), and 110 pounds, with watery black eyes and eyelashes that looked dipped in tar.

Continental was the new hip. There were outdoor café tables, an affectation from France. Also new and from France were green-glass bottles of Perrier adorning those tables, typically holding wildflowers. Suddenly everyone knew how to pronounce parmesan, edam, gouda. Woody Allen seduced Diane Keaton beside a platter of Rondelé. At home, we consumed low-rent, supermarket versions of the delicacies: powdered cappuccino, broccoli and brie in a bring-to-a-boil plastic sack. We told ourselves and everyone else that we were French.

In spite of its gourmet pretensions, this was New York at its nadir. There were strikes by garbage collectors, scaffolding removers, doormen, token-booth clerks. Laid-off cops rioted at the Brooklyn Bridge. It was the dark days of fiscal crisis, the era of "Ford to City: Drop Dead," the height of government layoffs, before the pooper scooper law, during days of drought and people yelling racial slurs at each other at top volume, and of the pushy, shovey New York— the rotting little island, as outsiders called it; the cesspool, as our father called it; "Fear City," as it was memorialized on a T-shirt that a friend used to wear; the place your life "wasn't worth a nickel," as one of our mother's boyfriends used to call our fine city.

In the universe of my dreams, I am, now, the same age as my mother, then. Our story takes place in a timeless in-between, metaphysically breaking the rules of nature. In this imagined place where no one ages, my mother and I could be sisters or best friends. This is what she always wanted. *Okay, here you have it: the prime of life, the prime of our lives.* Time collapses, the generation between us is elided.

I have a photograph of my mother from that period, taken by a fashion photographer during a break on one of her modeling shoots; she gave me as a gift not so many years ago to mark my age and match it to hers. She wears a man's mechanic's jacket, zipped up, with her hair silky and glossed, swept around her cheekbones and unstyled. She looks down, so as to accentuate the arresting clarity of her bone structure. She is stunning.

When we moved to New York, what held my attention first was celebrities in our building—the Rodney Dangerfields, whose daughter, Melanie, was my age, and the Carolyn Kennedy–David Nixon power duo. Brooke Shields was ever present in the neighborhood and on the bus ads. Also our neighbor was Mason Reese, the child actor, close to my age, known for his short stature, red hair, and his line in the Dunkin Donuts commercial: *This is what a munchkin looks like!*

What I recognized in the display was what was withheld from us, what gave us the impression we didn't belong—our fatherless threesome, cash poor. Perhaps there were others in our building who fell behind in the rent as soon as they got there. I don't actually know.

The celebrities attended private school, but there was also a lower social rung in our neighborhood and in our building, and its kids attended a well-rated public elementary school across the street. I went to that school too, but I seemed to belong to an even lower social rung.

Our building accounted for the largest single demographic of students at the elementary school, and it took up a whole block. With the pretension intrinsic to the moment, it had been named the Pavilion—it was just a decade old when we got there. In a survey of momentous New York City architecture, the architecture critic for the *Times*, Paul Goldberger, condemned it as the first in a wave of "white brick block-blusters" causing blight upon the eastern avenues of uptown. It had a grocery, a valet, a coiffeur, and an electronics store. It had its own zip code and its own catacombs of behind-the-lobby hallways stretching between six elevator banks to three separate towers, each with its own system of terraces and stairwells in which to play hide-and-seek and get lost and have dreams about, dreams in which one can never get home, like Kafka's Karl Rossmann taking too many unconsidered turns inside the labyrinth.

I no longer have that dream about getting lost in the labyrinth. Nor do I have an old recurring nightmare about an intruder coming through the front door, which we, like many in our building, were in the habit of leaving unlocked. The only dream I seem to have lately is about moving back in.

Now, Jill evokes for me, in lurid, amusing detail, a situation concerning their laundry at the apartment in Long Island City. It has been piling up for months, she says. It's possible. I haven't been coming in when I've seen my mother, meeting her outdoors because a long time ago I got in the habit of avoiding Jill this way. Rather than haul their clothes to the laundromat, they get new ones for free through Jill's outpatient rehab program at Bellevue. When Jill tells me this, I imagine them climbing over squalid heaps of dirty clothes to get from bedroom to bathroom.

I find myself actively avoiding the inside for fear of what I will find there. I envision a situation comparable to that of the hermit Collyer brothers of Harlem—living amid 120 tons of debris and fourteen grand pianos. I recently learned about this on National Public Radio. "The house was labyrinthine," according to a court order for its demolition in 1947, "with tiny passages between towers of stacked books, boxes, papers." Maybe Jill heard this too. Authorities discovered the detritus of the Collyer brothers' domestic existence once the brothers had passed away inside, with "Langley, dead about a month, decomposing under a crushing stack of newspapers, apparently a trap gone wrong. He lay about ten feet from where his brother, left without his caretaker, had died." This is, more or less, what I am imagining for my sister and my mother.

But no. When I finally go over, I see that their two beds are made up like army cots, the blankets taut. Two laundry bags are neatly tied up at the door. There are clean socks and underwear drying on a line in the bathroom. There are notes on stickies on the counters, the refrigerator door, the desk: *To go outside—1 keys + 2 cell phone* (items highlighted in yellow). There is a page with an empty circle drawn in its center. *To take in AM,* it reads underneath, for pills.

Jill writes these reminders in heavy ink or pencil lead, as if she is pushing hard into the page to make sure it doesn't escape from her, this line she is inscribing, as if she is afraid it will get forgotten, of its own accord, while she is in the middle of transmitting it through her neck and shoulders and arms and fingers. All her life she has suffered painful shoulder dislocations. Writing vigorously like this would do the job fine, I think. Her notes use the full range of tools available to the scribbler: caps, italics, underlines, highlights in yellow. These flourishes also adorn bills and receipts that Jill delivers to me these days, some so scrawled over I can't read what they say or use them effectively for reimbursements from a trust I have set up in order to qualify our mother for Medicaid.

I have organized our mother's finances according to a complicated, scaffolding-like> structure. Order gives us respite from worry. "In time of trouble, I had been trained since childhood, read, work it up, go to the literature," writes Joan Didion. "Information was comfort." There are now three bank accounts to facilitate a system of reimbursements and loans and shuttling of income required for Medicaid. This owes to a loophole in the law that I could explain right here except it took me three months to understand myself. I look over the receipts and imagine I am everybody's father.

For one year, our father paid for Jill to attend the Nightingale Bamford School for Girls, most famous lately as Gwyneth Paltrow's alma mater. Unlike my public elementary school, our local public junior high was not well rated, though eventually Jill and I both went to it anyway. At Nightingale Bamford, a fancy set took Jill in, and at their center was Chevy Chase's kid sister. Therefore, we were *Saturday Night Live* acolytes from the beginning: first show, first season. His sister, Nana, became an honorary member of our household, and though neither my mother nor I ever met her brother, we always called him "Chevy"—for instance, in comments such as "Chevy broke his back on that fall," or "Chevy got on pills for his back," or "Chevy's in for rehab now."

Though we were poor, our worldview was through the lens of the rich and the insulated. We could thank Chevy for what we knew of other existences. Today, it seems to me there was a thick slab of glass separating what we took in about our city then and history's version of New York in the 1970s. We followed the news on "Weekend Update with Chevy Chase." For this reason only, we knew that there was terrorism in Croatia:

> *And where did they hide their guns? And who made their little masks for them? How could these little crustaceans steal a plane?*
> *Miss Litella, that was Croatians. Five Croatians hijacked a plane. Croatians, not crustaceans.*
> *Oh. What are Croatians?*
> *Another kind of shellfish, Miss Litella.*

And in Denmark, reported Chevy, Sammy Davis, Jr., would be meeting with a surgeon:

> *. . . to discuss plans to undergo an operation to have his jewels removed.*

And about New York:

> *In New York this week, Ramsey Clark, Paul O'Dwyer, Bella Abzug, Daniel Patrick Moynihan and [pause] Abe Hirschfeld.*

We lost track of what went on around us, had perhaps lost ourselves in that same whisper of giggling and romance that had overtaken the city. It was not a part of our worldview to recognize that just over the bridge in Bushwick,

Brooklyn, there was an epidemic of insurance-related arson fires so pronounced that whole blocks had gone missing. Across a sweep of landscape, there was nothing to rest the eyes on but churches.

We never left Manhattan except to see family in Boston. On the Amtrak for semi-weekly custody visits with our father, Jill and I peered out as we rattled past buildings with burnt-out windows and char marks in the South Bronx, or at abandoned factories along the eastern seaboard with giant-sized product replicas on their rooftops: a Swingline stapler, a pack of Lifesavers. We didn't know what to make of all this economic collapse, didn't know how it connected to either of the two lives we crossed between in Boston and Manhattan. Today, I read about how the TV stations looped images of mayhem from the 1977 blackout: mobs hurtling through darkness; looters stabbing each other in tussles over a refrigerator or a TV set; four men wrenching a parking meter from the ground and using it to smash the window of a jewelry store. I watch this on YouTube.

About that fateful summertime week of the blackout, I remember only that Jill and I were up in Boston, and that we spoke to our mother on the telephone to hear how she'd fared on Seventy-seventh Street. She'd walked up the stairs to get home, our mother reported to us. Fifteen flights!

My mother and I go outside, toward our regular lunch spot downstairs from the apartment in Queens. The subway station is one stop over the river from Manhattan on the 7 line, two stops from my apartment in the East Village. Her tooth has been pulled. There was no sepsis.

"What would you like to do?" she offers.

"We were going to lunch," I remind her. We do this all the time.

"Really? Do you have any money? Because I don't have any money." We also have this conversation all the time—since I took over managing the money.

"Don't worry, I'll take you. With your money."

"Oh, okay! I'm really in bad shape. My memory. . . ." She trails off. "Don't worry, though," she assures me.

"I know," I say. She remembers me; she believes she will always remember me. But actually, the situation gives me an odd sense of dislocation, as if my disappearing from my mother's consciousness will coincide with my actually disappearing in real life. The foggier she becomes, the more I feel lost in fog and murk.

My nostalgia is reaching the point of compulsion—that is what I mean to say. Popular culture doesn't help me, with its endless respooling of *Manhattan* and *Annie Hall*. The latter played in Bryant Park recently. I watched, sitting alone, trying to transpose this refurbished Bryant Park into my memory of it, when junkies and rats ruled the walkways. The media seem to yearn as much as I do for New York City in that moment of transition, before Giuliani got out his Teflon. My longing doesn't fade. Just when I think I've gotten past it, there it turns up again like an old boyfriend who's stuck around the neighborhood long past when he should have quit.

Contrary to all manner of doomsday updates from Jill, health seems to exude from my mother's clear eyes and skin. At lunch, she is saying things like "I don't feel that—" making a hand gesture, reaching out and grasping, waiting for me to help her out. Plaques and tangles afflict different people in different parts of their prefrontal cortices. Every time she loses a word, I imagine a fleck of her brain has sloughed away.

"Desire?"

"Yes, desire. I'm not thinking about the past, not comparing this that I have now to something that was maybe different, or better or worse, before. I am just—" She purses her lips and looks far off and pushes a straight arm forward as if imitating a race car hurtling ahead.

"—concentrating on now?"

"Yes, concentrating on now."

These days I feel a kind of awe and respect that I used to experience in the presence of B. K. S. Iyengar in India. The guru would sit across his desk from me in his library exuding a nameless thing so simple and bright and joyful I couldn't grasp it in my mind as a palpable quality. It was pure life—pure living—uncomplicated by want. *Nirguna*, it seemed to be—without qualities—a term that also describes a state of transcendence. Transcendence is luminous—*amanaska*, perhaps, like those walls—and yet also empty—*nirguna*, I am thinking, a peaceful kind of empty.

When I don't feel awe I feel bafflement. It's hard to tell which version of the situation is true: the one I perceive when I'm with my mother, or Jill's. Often I think there is something crazy going on in that apartment in Long Island City. I will never find out about it until the two are discovered buried there beneath a pile of belongings.

I concoct scenarios to describe the space between what one or the other of them reports, the something-else scenario that I haven't the imagination to conceive of: the swerve—right there in front of me, so darkly invisible. It is as if there were a floor beneath me, but it is not really a floor, and I am dangling in midair, only I don't know it, and I won't know it until I look down at that floor and see that it isn't there at all, at which point I will drop, suddenly and windlessly.

What if everything I think is, isn't? My own reading of things could easily be a matter of *viparyaya*—erroneous interpretation. Neither Jill nor my mother is a reliable narrator.

Patañjali's yoga sutras concern themselves in large part with the skill of discerning truth—*pramana*—given the many layers of deception and delusion one encounters in one's own mind and in others. Yoga is an art of seeing clearly.

Who is doing the deceiving? My mother, or Jill, or that part of me that wants our past back?

"*What?*" my mother is pressing me, at lunch, as if it's someone else's fault that she doesn't understand, as if it's not fair, this situation, as if the world has played a mean trick on her.

I am trying to explain receipts. "In order to keep your Medicaid, you have to submit . . ." I repeat.

"What?" Her eyes say to me, *How dare you?*

"You need Medicaid in order to go to the senior center." The real answer is I want her to have Medicaid so that if and when Jill bails or flames out, a system will be in place for my mother to move somewhere else, or to receive long-term care, or to find full-time home care, paid for. I don't say any of this explicitly. I also avoid correcting the euphemism that has fallen into the everyday speech of our family: *the senior center.* It's adult day care—there is a bold sign emblazoned with the phrase on the entryway to the very building. She was rejected from a free day program at a senior center where I brought her one day, close to her apartment on Queens Boulevard. "Your mother is not appropriate for our level of care. She needs full-time, one-to-one supervision," said a harried social worker who called me in crisis later in the day. I don't remind my mother about this.

"I'm afraid she's unlikely to see eighty," Jill wrote in a text to me recently, replying to a note in which I warned that their spending was running over our budget. There was a monthly amount we could take out if we wanted her savings to last until she was eighty-two, according to a man at her retirement fund. And they were spending too much.

I think a lot about what will happen when our mother dies. The life expectancy after diagnosis with Alzheimer's is five to ten years. Jill and I heard that and immediately dismissed it. Not our mother. She was diagnosed at sixty-seven. She'd said on several occasions, earlier in life, that she planned to live to ninety-nine, and there was never a reason to doubt this. Her mother lived for ninety-four years, soused on liquor for seventy-five of them. What will happen to Jill?

Two days ago, a storm dumped nearly a foot of snow on our city. It is still thick, plowed or salted along walkways, and there are exhaust-grayed mounds of snow-plow detritus lining the curbs. You can't bust through except where the steps of a thousand pedestrians have carved walkways at the crosswalks; it's that time of year you can't cross at the middle of a block without climbing a mountain to reach the sidewalk. My mother stares out the window of the café. I've tried to give her triggers about the day program—the food, the driver—but they've called up little, just pleasant associations about "the people," who are "very nice, very kind, I can't remember any of them, I can't see a face. But I think they're nice. Very kind." I can see she is thinking hard, trying to get a visual, when she says this.

"Look at the colors," she adds. More and more, this is what we can do. We talk about the colors we see. "The light's different. It's not always like this. Everything is so—"

I look hard. "Blue? It's bluer."

"Right."

And the asphalt is blacker, so black it's not even black anymore. More like silver. "And silver," I say.

"Right. And over there"—she points east—"the clouds are so, *slow.*"

"And still," I say, agreeing. It is not a bad way to spend an afternoon, I think, seeing colors in a new way.

The Oracle

We knew MacGraw, our mother's boyfriend then, mostly by what we didn't know. I eventually learned his first name, but I was pledged to secrecy on this count, as well as about which beautiful, then-popular movie actress from a highborn American family was his sister, from whom he was estranged. There was much else about him that was enigmatic—there seemed to be a lost fortune somewhere—and even the facts I did glean had been hard won. He kept his birthday a secret, though I recall my mother discovered the date in order to determine his sign, which I think was Sagittarius.

What he lacked in the tangible he made up for in graces—physical beauty and charisma and regal bearing, and gifts, items seemingly culled from a Mughal princedom. These were often sculpted from peacock feathers that he gathered in the cemetery at the Cathedral of Saint John the Divine, near an SRO where he lived on Upper Broadway. Sapristi, a mythical African priestess, was the name he gave my mother. One of his gifts to her was this name spelled out in the feathers, on a plaque made from mat board. It was shaped like a fish, reference to an object in Bob McKee's den in Westport: an iridescent, five-foot marlin, embalmed and mounted beside a photo of my stepfather holding the fish on its hook on a boat in Florida.

MacGraw praised my mother's every creative gesture—acting, painting, singing—in hers and anyone else's presence. She was an artist, he said. And in truth she was, though more in spirit than in fact: a master of personas, a fashion model.

This all caused Jill to go ranting about the apartment railing against our mother: *Prima donna. Prima donna.*

MacGraw also smelled, like stale sweat and cigarettes—the Camel non-filters that stained his knuckles and long fingernails. A friend of our mother's often made the criticism that he didn't bathe, which was probably true since he did live in that SRO. He regaled us with tales of it, of cloak-and-dagger eviction tactics by a slumlord who wanted to convert the building to student apartments and lease them to Columbia University. One day there was a suspicious oven fire; on another an aged neighbor turned up inexplicably dead.

MacGraw had no job: his stated profession was "inventor." The pungency of his smell also likely derived from the fact he owned only one set of clothing: brown corduroys, a black button-down dress shirt, a woven blazer, a black overcoat, and a woven black-wool scarf. In our apartment, he often wore only black boxers so that he could work on his life-long project of repairing the cords, or, with his pants on, the other items. He rewove the cords rent by rent, using matching brown thread and two needles.

My mother says he was her one true love and gets weepy now when I bring him up. "He's dead," she says with certainty. "Probably dead. I think so. Dead." She looks off to a middle distance, lost, or not lost, it's hard to say. I notice how beautiful she is, and think of a Velázquez painting I saw in Spain once of the oracle at Delphi.

We are eating together at a glamorous caviar bar on Seventh Avenue, and she is doing that thing she does—disappearing for a second, as if she's had a stroke. *I'm thinking*! Why so defensive? Was she really, actually, dropping out from our shared world, shifting to a consciousness held privately by her alone?

Now she shifts back again. As usual, I am relieved that I waited for her to come back, that I didn't try to jar her into our world by asking my question again and calling her attention to her lapse from reality.

"It's too bad it couldn't lead to anything," she says, returning to MacGraw. "I knew it couldn't, but I couldn't end it either." She doesn't remember, now, how they broke up. She's better reflecting on *feel,* the palpable sense-memories of the past, rather than fact or detail. "It was too bad he was so"—she pauses—"*wacky.*" Sometimes she says *wicky,* but I know she means *wacky* now. *Wicky* is her made-up word to remind the listener, who already knows, that she is losing her memory. It means, roughly, Alzheimer's-ish. But Mac-Graw actually was *wacky.* "It never felt *real,*" she continues, about MacGraw.

What is real? Where does my mother go when she goes to that place? It is not an Alzheimer's place. It is a my-mother place, that's always been there for her.

I think what she means is that MacGraw couldn't take care of himself, hadn't figured out how to sustain himself, much less help us negotiate the enormous, daunting work it cost us to live our lives then. My mother makes a body gesture, as if creating a solid ground on which to squat or sit cross-legged. Her physical expressiveness lent her naturally to her career in fashion modeling. "Yes," I say, filling in blanks for her. MacGraw was a man more of the ethers, up there with his twirling exhales of cigarette smoke. I do think he was a Sagittarius—fire—but certainly with a moon in something airy.

My mother met MacGraw out in public, which also contributed to our sense of him as evanescent and unrooted. We didn't have roots ourselves—being new in the city, not knowing anyone aside from her best modeling friend, Rusty. Our mother met MacGraw when she was out with Rusty one late-summer evening at an outdoor café across from Lincoln Center.

He'd probably been walking by—it's unlikely he was a customer as he not only had no income but objected to restaurants on the ideological ground of anti-materialism.

I picture him stopped dead in his tracks by the beauty emanating from that table, my mother and Rusty likely sipping Perrier, dressed in flowing diaphanous things. Maybe he even described that scene for us once—*stopped dead in my tracks.* That was his style of Depression era hobo speech; it was a little Midwestern, giving faint hints of where he'd come from, how he'd got here. My mother, the mystic, would have been the more susceptible of the two to his charms. Or she was the more beautiful—I remember she was, but of course I am biased. I imagine he handed my mother a peacock feather.

That is what he did the first time he came to our apartment, one night shortly after my eleventh birthday. He was wastrel thin, with long charcoal hair, a sparse Confucian beard, and delicate high cheekbones. His hands were handsome, like a piano player's, strong and sensitive, long and sinewy. If he had been less than six foot three he would have appeared unmanly, but he was at least that tall, and he had broad, angular shoulders and sensitive, peacock-shaped, sapphire-colored eyes with prominent lashes.

Also, as my mother says to me now in her snapshot of him, apparently forgetting for a second to whom she is speaking, "He was good with my girls. He loved my girls." It is as if I have bifurcated into two *me*'s for my mother: me now, and me then. I do remember he taught me things: how to cross the avenue in dense traffic by walking at a sharp angle to the moving taxicabs; how to barter for a free Christmas tree late at night on Christmas Eve; how to do something he said was *to look* but actually meant *to really see*.

I also remember he had beautiful wrists, and I remember looking at them that evening as he took an unmarked and unsealed white business envelope from the pocket of his overcoat and passed it to my mother. Pieces of iridescent fuzz emerged from the envelope, which upon being fully extracted revealed themselves as feathers from the underside of a young peacock. Their provenance, MacGraw explained, was the churchyard around the corner from his SRO, at Saint John the Divine. Here, there were peacocks running loose. We could visit the churchyard with him, which we certainly would (though we would never see the inside of his fabled SRO, that lurid place so vivid in those tales brought back for us).

I recall that he had an overcoat, though it was late summer or early fall. But this is not out of keeping with who he was. Later, we knew him to wear that overcoat during all seasons, for a reason I don't remember specifically but that was, I think, connected to his poverty—for instance, wanting to cover the clothes underneath out of shame, or to make sure the coat wasn't stolen. He also wore tai chi slippers, the kind made of black canvas with thin, orange, rubber soles that you could buy in Chinatown for three dollars. These were also a part of his uniform no matter the season, no matter the level of precipitation or dense snow or frigid temperature.

On this night he carried a brown paper bag with a book inside and one of those crinkly orange plastic sacks so abundant in Chinatown. The book was a copy of the I Ching, which we already possessed in our household but in a different translation, and in the bag was a pack of bamboo sticks, about the size of shish kebob skewers, in a plastic wrapper adorned with Chinese characters.

We were in the habit of practicing the I Ching by throwing three coins—usually pennies—but according to Mac-Graw the more traditional method required the random laying down of fifty sticks of yarrow, or bamboo if you couldn't find yarrow. MacGraw's instructions, he said, came from a "wise old son of a bitch" in a stall on a twisty street in Chinatown. In my memory I have a clear picture of that stall, though I don't think I actually saw it in particular. It had a red paper lantern, octagonal and swinging from an exposed electrical cord that snaked across a low ceiling. Pipes showed along the concrete up above, and, possibly on this visit (or an imagined visit), a rat skittered through.

MacGraw and my mother went off to her bedroom—her "cave," she called it, because it was painted a velvety charcoal. When they emerged they had the book wrapped in a square of Chinese silk. They unwrapped it and laid it, on top of the silk, on our living room table, and then announced that the person doing the reading must face south, or toward the door to our building's hallway, and the consultee north, in the direction of our windows. Our apartment consisted of this small, box-shaped living room and a single bedroom off to the side. There was also a galley kitchen, generally cluttered with dirty dishes and where all the drawers had come off their runners: none of us knew, yet, how to fix them, though eventually I taught myself this skill.

For the first session, I believe, my mother faced the hallway and I the window, though I don't remember my question. Whatever it was, it was unlikely to have been a question I actually cared about, as I would have been ashamed to ask in front of them: *Will I be like you? Will I be beautiful?* Jill had many impressive friends who invited her to stunning apartments nearby. Maybe I asked if I would be like Jill in a year or two, or at least if her friends would like me.

We then spent the evening rotating seats. Again and again, we threw the bamboo sticks and examined the arrangements, the angles and shapes and the meaning of those random single sticks that sometimes landed apart from the pile. One of the tosses, perhaps, called up the hexagram Hsu that night, the symbol of waiting (water over sky):

It will be advantageous to cross the great stream. Clouds rise up to heaven.

The caviar bar is Petrossian, and my mother and I have come to celebrate Christmas Eve. Jill has stayed home in bed, with a migraine or just a bad mood. I choose our dishes—steak tartare for my mother, smoked salmon for me, Stilton and arugula salad for both of us. Petrossian is art déco in design, Francophilic and Russian in menu, and housed in a famous building around the corner from Carnegie Hall with a façade so ornate that it is often referred to as the "wedding cake building." I have ordered us tickets for tonight at Carnegie—a program I know she'll love including Bach's *Concerto for Three Violins in D Major.*

In this pre-performance hour the restaurant is empty, and in spite of the tables I choose the bar for our meal because we can sit close and speak in whispers. It is a spacious bar, with gold-tinted mirrors that reflect the sleek lines of the interior. My mother will be comfortable here, owing to the mirrors. To have Alzheimer's is to have to always be vigilant, to remember to check your back, check your pockets. *Keys? Cell phone? MetroCard?*

After a time, we are joined at the bar by the occasional diner also building a meal off the caviar menu: a man in a silk cravat and leather-soled shoes; two older women sipping from champagne flutes and eating toasts; a couple who exhibit the kind of easy intimacy that doesn't require conversation. I imagine these are people for whom a nighttime concert at Carnegie Hall might be a daily activity. My mother and I spend a few minutes reading significances into their clothing and gestures. This is what we've always done. I say they remind me of the extras in French movies from the sixties.

"Oh, really? Which?"

"Vincente Minnelli," I say, knowing she won't get the reference but that she wouldn't if it were Bardot either. "Do you remember Jane Fonda?" I add.

She gets misty and far away. "Yes," she says after a while.

Later, she says she has to go to the bathroom.

"Are you okay?" I know she won't be. I let her go anyway, certain that in five minutes I will get up and look for her, and that I will discover her wandering around the empty restaurant with a dazed, in-the-moment, take-it-as-it-comes expression.

"She has Alzheimer's," I say matter-of-factly to the bartender after she leaves. She is still slender. Dressed in velvets and silks tonight, she looks like someone important and self-possessed. The bartender goes blank, as if I've said something in another language.

When we take our stools at the bar again, my mother asks for the hundredth time today about the men in my life, and I tell her the same things I've already said a hundred times earlier today. I'm happy to go over it aloud with her, though. She picks up on details. "Good!" she'll exclaim, or "Oh that's not good"—frowning—or "No, that won't work."

"How do you imagine the perfect man?" I ask her after a while.

"A best friend."

"That's nice." This conversation between us is always spoken with the understanding that neither of us has had a successful, lasting, romantic relationship in our lives. The hypothetical notion of finding a true love and staying with him, the impossible dreaming, is what makes this conversation so delicious.

"What about sex?" I counter. "Best friends without sex, is that perfect?"

"Oh, no." She purses her lips. "You're right. That's really important, too." She sighs and looks off, gets dreamy-eyed again.

"Were you best friends with MacGraw?"

"That's so funny you would ask that. That's a very good question. Yes. And physically. We were good. It's too bad—" She always acts surprised lately when I have followed her line of thinking, though usually I have planted the idea in her head to begin with, only she's forgotten the prompt, now faded into a past that is three or four or seven minutes long.

Conversations about appealing men are generally connected to talk of her father—for instance, about how lucky she was to have a father who was such a good man. "And he was handsome too," she adds. "Have you ever known any men like that?"

"Sure," I say, grinning. I know that in her mind she's made a segue back to her father. "Your father."

After we met MacGraw, it became a practice in our family to try to *see*. Learning to see required learning to un-see, first. The un-seeing was something you could get good at. We tried to blank out our minds, and then *look*. "The darkness of the day" was an expression MacGraw used sometimes. He'd gotten it from Carlos Castaneda. The "darkness of the day," said the mystic Yaqui Don Juan, was the best time to see. "You don't see. . . . You only look at the surface of things," said Don Juan, castigating his charge.

When my mother has those silent lapses, *looking* is ostensibly what she is doing, or, rather, she is *un*-looking, in preparation to look. She is taking the time it requires to relax her mind sufficiently for it to let go of its preconceived thoughts and visions. Then she will be able to see clearly.

Taking them in early, I internalized these techniques of seeing and un-seeing, perhaps in the deep, intuitive manner of a child learning a new language. It does seem to me a language I learned. I also received training in actual art, encouraged by my mother during those years she called herself an artist because she was beautiful, and when MacGraw went along with her, and when Jill, not exactly understanding the very aptness of the expression, called our mother *prima donna*.

One year, my mother and I convinced my father to pay for classes for me at the prestigious Art Students' League, though what he did was deduct from his child support to pay for them. I'd shown a talent, goes the lore, inherited from our grandmaman. One year for Christmas, my mother bought me *Drawing on the Right Side of the Brain*, by Betty Edwards, which I read cover to cover, and re-read, and re-read again while practicing the exercises.

Edwards spoke of "right-hemisphere mode." This was the "intuitive, subjective, relational, holistic, time-free mode." Left-brain mode involved "drawing symbolic shapes from memory." The right brain saw in a manner "different-from-ordinary," and was of course the preferred mode for the artist.

So I understand what she is talking about, this landscape painter I've recently met, when she tells me that she is in the habit of looking at her paintings reflected in a hand mirror. She stands far away, with her back to the painting, and situates her painting in the reflection. This reversal knocks out the path of neurons accustomed to seeing it in the old way. She was also taught, in art school, to look at her paintings in the dark, "so you can see form"—which sounds to me a bit like the "daytime darkness" MacGraw used to talk about.

Long after they parted, I started to bump into MacGraw from time to time on Upper Broadway. This was in the early nineties, more than a decade after my mother first met him. He was still wearing those same clothes, though the actual threads seemed to have gone through several cycles of regeneration.

I was attending Columbia University at the time, where a classmate of mine, who lived in university housing, once identified MacGraw to me as one of the "homeless people" who lived in his building. *An oxymoron?* I thought bitterly. The university was trying to evict this crew in order to complete its conversion of that property to student rentals. This sounded just right—MacGraw had told us those stories.

The first time I saw MacGraw, I stopped him, and we hugged warmly and looked into each other's eyes. It had been seven or eight years. Time had not treated him well. The way he huddled into his overcoat and carried grocery bags filled with belongings could certainly create that impression he was homeless.

As the weather got colder that winter, MacGraw shrank more and more inside that old overcoat. Several times when I saw him he didn't recognize me, and while I tried to make eye contact, I also often let him pass as I was carried along by a wave of friends from school or a sweep of new responsibilities.

What I noticed looking into his eyes on that first day on Broadway was their expression of wisdom, but also a cloudiness, a bleary quality. They were blue, very pale. I had a moment of uncertainty about the oracles.

Then MacGraw looked into the sky and pointed out that it would be a full moon that night. "Go look at the moon tonight," he told me. It was just beginning to snow, and the avenues had that expectant, optimistic feel they get in early winter. They smelled of wetness and fresh life. "Make sure you go outside, get away from the streetlights, and look up. Don't forget to look up. Make sure you really see."

I am jarred from this memory as the bartender at Petrossian slides behind the bar and makes a gesture toward our plates.

My mother bats her eyes at him and places her still-full wine glass on her empty steak tartare dish. She turns to me. Mom is still the best date ever, I think. "Shall we order some food now, honey?" she suggests.

"We just ate." I say.

"Really? Was it good?"

It is mercifully warm this Christmas Eve. Later, my mother and I lock arms and stroll down the block to the concert hall. "This sacred place," tonight's conductor has described Carnegie Hall, in an interview in the program notes. The space does feel that way; the bright red velvet of the upholstery and seating is offset by red silk tops on many of the female members of the orchestra, and audience members have dressed in a preponderance of red hats and scarves as well, as if by design. The musical theme of the evening is fugue: first, a work for strings by a twentieth-century composer, Edward Elgar, based on a Welsh folk tune—"a devil of a fugue," in the composer's own words; then the Bach—its final movement, the program notes reminding us, being "densely fugal."

The music puts me into a fugue state myself. Those moments from our past swirl in my head, less as stories than as images, smells, sense-memories, emotions. My mother seems to be transported, sitting next to me, intently watching the orchestra. We used to have Wassily Kandinsky's *Concerning the Spiritual in Art* in our bookshelf, beside our I Chings and tarot decks. Color, shape, and music, Kandinsky wrote, could communicate our innermost spiritual and psychological concerns. Through a "power of inner suggestion," abstraction creates a "spiritual atmosphere," a "psychic effect."

Then I notice a scent, then a flash of green amid the red, then a wash of joy, and a wash of pain, and a wash of nostalgia.

I saw MacGraw less and less, his condition worsening each time. At the last, I specifically noticed that his clothes were the very same he used to wear, rewoven at every stitch. They were like a ghost, a sheath of their former selves. In spite of the cold, he also still wore canvas tai chi slippers, though maybe a newer pair in this case.

Then, after a while, MacGraw really did disappear, just like my mother said.

Bombing the Ghost

The girls from Harlem used to corn-row Freddi's long, silky hair for him in class. Once he left a note for me in marker on the mailbox outside our building, his script white on the blue box: TO LIZ ▪ FREDDI. Then he gave me an LP tagged and pieced up on the liner sleeve with cartoon images of himself and me gazing in amazement at the beauty and large size and bright colors of his lettering.

Freddi took me bombing with his crew one night, Darkside Artists (DSA), with Anthem and Shark, some other girls too—Psyche, I think, and a few who didn't tag. We entered the tunnel at the north end of the Eighty-sixth and Broadway station and walked on a thin ledge, at platform level, a block or so to the southern edge of the ghost station: "91," read the old mosaic letter work. The guys were dressed alike in long wool army coats and carried messenger bags heavy with their spray cans. It was 2 A.M., and there weren't supposed to be many trains.

Sharkie had prepped us in case there were. One came while we'd been in the tunnel between stations. We hurled ourselves against the wall and made ourselves thin in that narrow width of ledge, like two-D cartoon characters. I felt a thrill at the speed and energy of that stream of subway cars, that endless one-against-the-next hurtling so fast.

"Stand clear the sizzling mainline," Shark had warned us also, about the third rail. I wasn't scared. The subways felt to me like that kind of a machine you operate so often it's as if it's a piece of your body. My bicycle felt that way too. Maybe my mother's sewing machine felt that way to her. Maybe for Jill it was her guitar. Jill's and my subway stop for Stuy High was on a curve, so there was a metal grating that shifted outward to connect the platform to the subway car when the train arrived at the station. "Stand clear the moving platform," an announcer said. Shark's phrase was a play on that.

Sharkie had the mouth. "Make yo'self slenda'," he instructed us. "Slenda' like Donni"—meaning Donni the comics character, not Dondi, the bomber who was up everywhere, but playing the pun. Sharkie talked like he was black, but he was five-foot-three with hair like the Gerber baby's and eyes, we used to say, that were red, white, and blue. DSA was mostly white. "Anybody got cash-ish?" he'd say, or he'd comment, if anyone asked, that he and I knew each other because we were "spoons" together, by which he meant Stuyvesant kids who hung out smoking pot outside Tony's, the greasy spoon on Fifteenth Street, during lunch or after school or while we were cutting.

Sharkie and I lived on the same train line. It was always rush hour, and inside the cars there were always men leering, drooling, and groping. Sharkie taught me how to climb on between cars. Rush hour was so bad that a lot of times the train left behind a platform full of commuters, leerers, lurkers. You pulled back a spring-loaded metal divider between the two cars, then lifted a vertical metal bar out of a U-frame that connected a row of three horizontal chains. Then, holding onto the bar with the chains, you stepped onto the rusted metal outer platform at the head of one of the two facing cars and reconnected the crossbar from there. Sharkie and I would stand across from each other, one on each of the two car ledges.

This activity infuriated the train conductors and transit police, so you had to "make yo'self stealth," as Sharkie said. Every once in a while a transit cop came running for me across the crowded platform just as the train was pulling out, and we smiled and waved goodbye at him. "La-tah fo' you," gloated Sharkie.

Sharkie was always smoking a joint when I saw him on the train. "Yo, sistah,"—cough, cough, exhale—"make yo'self slim. Thin like Donni. Transit cop 'most caught you by the locks"—which long hair Shark then touched, and I shrank away because Sharkie was half my height. On those days I showed up at classes stoned, and if I bumped into Sharkie at lunch at Tony's we went to Stuy Park and smoked more.

"I'd rather know you're doing it someplace safe," said Jill's and my mother, about drugs, by which she meant we could party at our place. She wanted to see things from the inside out.

The night we bombed the ghost, when I came home my mother was tripping.

We got to the station. It looked nearly like a functioning one, but abandoned and unlit it made me feel out of my body, as if I were looking down on a dream I'd had. I was living in a post-apocalyptic future, but also a time I could almost look back on already.

Most of the girls watched while the boys and Psyche worked fast with spray cans. The images were black and gray and rounded; in the dark it was hard to make out what made them pretty. Freddi was the talent. He was making a precise outline, which the boys teased him for. Freddi had a messenger bag of about two dozen bright colors of spray paint, but that night no one got past the second color because we heard something in the tracks. Probably a rat. We sidled along the ledge again and exited the station back at Eighty-sixth. Coming up to Broadway into a flat, pre-dawn glare, we must have seemed like underground creatures, and I felt as if there were a whole secret subterranean world we occupied and no one knew what lurked there but us. It felt intimate, secret, ours.

Afterwards, we walked the three blocks to Central Park and watched the sun rise in a sky so pale and purple that the sun looked like a moon. We went out of our way to get back via the local so we could watch that ghost from inside a subway car and see what the commuters would see tomorrow. The station wasn't much, still underground-black, the platform grimy and littered with slips of refuse, charcoal-covered and impossible to distinguish. It was just shapes and a creosote smell.

I rode home from Freddi's on my bike. I felt like wind, flying through orange air, racing into the sunrise.

When I came home the sun was just up. My mother was sitting on the sofa with the cat, the lights still on. Her eyes were glassy. I'd noticed with my girlfriends and myself that taking acid made us more beautiful, our skin dewier and our cheeks pinker. This was the case with my mother now. A project lay abandoned in the sewing machine on the other side of the room.

"Are you tripping?" I said. It was what you said when someone was obviously tripping, because otherwise they wouldn't tell you. Jill once spent a whole day with her boyfriend without his ever knowing. So you had to ask to find out; otherwise, they'd be playing a game on you.

My mother was whispering to the cat. "Look at this," she said, looking up at me. She gestured with her eyes to the cat's eyes.

"Yes?"

"Look." It was true the cat was gazing up at her with a hypnotized expression. "He trusts me completely."

There wasn't anything to indicate this wasn't the case. Our cat had a hair-trigger personality, sometimes fritzing out like he'd touched an electrical wire. Sometimes he chased Jill into the closet. The cat's eyes looked glassy now.

"Did you feed Cuckoo acid?"

"No."

"Did you take acid?"

"I always say if you guys are going to take drugs I'd rather you do it where I know you're safe. It was in the freezer. Look." She gestured back at the cat. "Watch this." She placed her pinky finger inside the cat's ear and gently screwed it in.

"I don't think that's a good idea."

She twisted her long hair behind her in a manner she seemed to have picked up from Jill, and then shook it out and peered back at the cat. "Cuckoo," she gently whispered, and then made cooing noises while the cat continued to gaze back at her, transfixed.

I go to the Strand this week and sit in the graffiti section for a long time, trying to fix an image of the pieces from that night—*Anthem, Shark, Freddi*. There is a wall of photo books on New York graffiti. Memory of DSA has not survived, but one of the books talks about Acid Writers, a crew we knew. These books are in the art section, near monographs by Jean-Michel Basquiat and Keith Haring. The information clerk has never heard of Haring. I want to shake her. That this work endures in the art section is testament to its enduring value. And yet her ignorance somehow obliterates it. What *is* its value?

I feel overwhelmed—sensory, so full and vital. I can't quite articulate to myself what the feeling is, can't find words for it. I have become aphasic, like my mother now, with emotions and sensations bigger than a vocabulary to express them with. Why does this feel so good? Am I the only one who feels it?

Back home that night, I watch *Downtown 81* for the fifth time, Glenn O'Brien's movie from the era with Jean-Michel Basquiat and Debbie Harry cast as leads. Most of the shots are at night. There is graffiti on every wall, squiggles that when I look hard turn into tags by people I knew. Basquiat's social circle overlapped with Jill's. There are nightclubs where my friends and I sneaked in—legal was eighteen, so you got in by looking fifteen. At Peppermint Lounge: Basquiat with his corkscrew dreads, held off at the velvet ropes.

I remember standing right there with Jill and her crowd—I think it was New Year's Eve exactly, 1981, me a sallow and shapeless fifteen. A boy told me I looked like Bianca, I looked like Brooke. I didn't feel that power, but I was buzzed, coming down from tripping, and the notion felt sparkly. He was already creating a mythology of us. We all were.

In *Downtown 81*, the camera lingers on a night scene around the corner from my current apartment, at Fourteenth Street and Second Avenue, also two blocks from the old Stuyvesant High. In the image is a neon banner: DISCO DONUT. It's a Kentucky Fried Chicken now. Trannies used to hang out there, just at the beginning of AIDS. That's what Sharkie called them, "trannies." Mornings when we came from the subway, the ladies sat in a gaggle at the curb drinking pop and slapping each other and talking in high voices. *Git that purple thang off yo' head!* one of them trash-talked Psyche once, because of her psychedelic scarf. *Git that purple thang off yo' head!* After that everyone greeted Psyche saying that.

There is a shot at a desolate Astor Place, facing down Lafayette onto what is a Walgreens now. The street is broad—imposing, empty. The buildings are large against an open sky. Today at that corner the buildings are cluttered against a skyscape dense with the wavy new postmoderns by Fumihiko Maki and Thom Mayne and Kazuyo Sejima. Until last year this was the corner of Starbucks and Starbucks; then the company got clear on business smarts and shut down the second one.

I want to set the images right, in the present. A moiré is making me dizzy, this overlay of then on now—all the different thens. I want to settle the visual, fix the now so it's sharp, not nausea-inducing, so it overtakes this persistent past.

How does one attach to the present when it is so constantly under construction? My maps keep getting remade. The MTA keeps configuring that iconic subway map in another new way, into a new icon, with routes that keep crisscrossing over the routes of the past, so quickly changing.

This summer there is a new M line. Why is it orange and not brown? Why is the M doing something completely different from what it used to do, acting like another version of the D? It's all wrong. But I know it will only seem wrong to me briefly. They've switched things up on us so often that we know we'll get past this problem of adjustment. We got over the conversion of the RR, the splitting of the NR, the dissolution of the QB. We adapt.

I finish watching the movie for the sixth and seventh times and then contact Anthem on Facebook. I ask him to fill in my memories from that night at the ghost.

He replies, saying he wasn't there, or at least in his memory he wasn't. He says it was probably just Shark and Freddi. But he remembers the art. He seems to think about that art a lot still. It was stunning, he says. DSA, he points out, has disappeared from cultural memory, ranking not a single hit on Google. "It saddens me that such a cool bit of history has been undocumented," he writes. "When Freddi granted me membership it was like I had won an Oscar or something."

He sends me images of art he's doing now. It's beautiful, in the same style as then—tags and pieces, but now on paper, or screen, not walls. "If there were movies of our high school years, would you watch them?" he asks me. "Or is reconstructing them more interesting?"

Swerve

Jill and our mother have this game. They stand at opposite ends of my mother's apartment tossing a superball to each other and watching the new cat, Cookie, chase it from the bedroom straight on through to the kitchen. This is especially fun because it's a railroad flat—four rooms strung together like carts on a track. Cookie runs back and forth. Again and again. It seems like no one will ever tire of this . . . until Jill does.

I'm watching the three of them do this and thinking of my student with the wandering eye last week hula-waving her eyes over to the side, along with her hands. She stared off into an invisible distance or distances as she used the word "swerve" to describe the technique in a short story we read in class. A swerve sidewinds the reader when it surfaces in a last, career-to-the-side-of-the-highway paragraph. The swerve is a relevant but different story, taking place on the shoulder of the road where you were too distracted to look for a real story.

This looking in the wrong place is also a kind of *viparyaya,* or error, I am thinking now as I watch the ball, followed by the cat, ricochet from one end to the other of the railroad flat. The swerve might even be an error of a higher phylum, such as *avidya*—misconception, or delusion. Swerve, *viparyaya, avidya,* I go on thinking and tuning out. *Viparyaya,* from Patañjali yoga, means delusion and basically suggests that it is impossible to see anything clearly unless one has stripped away all the veils of prejudice, hope, worry, traumatic memory, wishful thinking, and projection that clutter everyday experience. Then one is yogically enlightened. Until then, one is blinded by this tendency to think the real problem lies elsewhere when in fact it's directly in front of you, goading.

My mother loves me after all, for instance, even if she could never remember a damned thing about me. *I'm a vegetarian. I've been commuting to Penn State for a temporary teaching job. My ex and I broke up. If there's chicken in the ramen I don't eat it.* Now that we know memory was the problem and nothing passive aggressive, we also know that our mother will die. This awful disease will take her. Swerve.

With Jill staying in the apartment, my contribution is to repair the small things that are increasingly transforming to big things. It feels good to fix tangible problems when I can't stanch the mortal ones: atrophy, decay, slow death. My other duty is to spend several hours a week on the phone with Jill talking her down from crises.

Today: my mother didn't want to wash her hair. This is the problem I'm focused on now. I have brought fancy shampoos. *Where's the swerve?,* I think as I unpack the pleasingly shaped bottles onto the kitchen table while Jill watches and giggles. *Is it the hair?* Like any swerve I'll never see it or else it wouldn't be a swerve. "Doesn't this smell *nice?*" I say to our mother while mawking at Jill.

My mother sniffs one and gets an abstracted expression, concentrating hard. *"Lovely!* Oh, Lizzy, that is really nice. Peaches," she says.

After the memory problem and before the hair, my mind was on an overbearing social worker whom Jill and I call Miss Malaprop. She was phoning to tell me our mother would get lost if we left her at home alone or let her go out— "not that she's a prisoner or anything."

Our mother is a "wander risk." She likes to go walking— walking and walking, miles a day. Six months ago she went out and didn't come home. Jill called me in Pennsylvania after our mother had been gone for eight hours, and I called the cops, and Jill and I spent the rest of the night on the phone talking and crying together and calming each other down until 3 A.M., when a security guard noticed our mother walking back and forth, back and forth in the housing projects beneath the Queensborough Bridge.

After this, Malaprop insisted we increase surveillance. Jill couldn't put in more hours and keep going to her day program at Bellevue, so Malaprop agreed to help us out with the 24/7 situation by increasing the time our mother attended the Medicaid-funded daycare center—from 7 A.M. until the van dropped her off at home, anytime between one and three in the afternoon. Problem: solved.

This was good, because Jill hadn't looked so good to me lately, and she'd been complaining again about her chronic back pain. The Alzheimer's Association reports that more than 33 percent of family caregivers report symptoms of depression, but Jill came to the situation with that. She was in the habit of sending me text messages with signoffs such as *love, your psychologically very fragile sister Jill.* So I was relieved that Malaprop had offered up the increased hours to occupy our mother's daytimes.

Many obstacles seem to clear. The hair crisis averted, I go to yoga and accomplish galavasana to sirsasana to chaturanga. This includes an arm balance, and a headstand, and a thrilling leap through the air. I feel mastery. My body glides through space; I control each minuscule muscle movement. It's a hot summer day and, in the class, Frank, the teacher, says, "When it's about 98.6 degrees like this I feel like the air is meeting me, it's hugging me." I also believe that the universe is coming to meet me; it is watching out for me and my small family.

Later that day, Malaprop phones. "How are you, Elizabeth, how are you?" She is calling to deliver the next swerve. Malaprop is Malaprop because she speaks in clichés.

"Fine, thanks, Malaprop. How are you?" Actually, I call her by her real name. Malaprop likes to say my name so much that I offer hers as often as possible as well.

"Not so good, Elizabeth, not so good. The van has been waiting to drop off your mom for an hour and a half, Elizabeth. An hour and a half."

I'm in my apartment in the East Village, and the van has brought my mother to her apartment, twenty minutes from mine by subway. Jill is not there to receive her, is what Malaprop is saying. The tradeoff for Malaprop's daily daycare is that someone must be waiting at the flat in Long Island City when the center sends our mother home. Jill said she'd be home today. I meet the van sometimes, too, but not today.

"Elizabeth, you know we've had this problem before, Elizabeth." My mother and the van driver have been waiting on the sidewalk for an hour and a half. The driver keeps buzzing upstairs for Jill but no one answers. Jill has missed the van dropoff a dozen times already. Malaprop makes each of these statements three times.

They're cutting us off, Malaprop adds. *Swerve*. This statement startles me so much that I ignore it. They're kicking our mother out of the day program, Malaprop repeats, because Jill has missed the van too many times. Malaprop repeats her statement a third time, and then a fourth and fifth, so I can no longer ignore it. I recognize that a new order of problem has entered.

On the other hand, by the time I get off the subway in Long Island City twenty minutes later, my mind has moved past the current obstacle and projected itself to the next one. I aim to complete an A/C installation that I began yesterday but couldn't finish because it turned out the socket was busted. I have a power strip to attach the new unit to a working outlet, foam to weatherstrip it, blue tape to cover the burned electrical plate. I'm not thinking of the inevitable swerve really—for instance, where is Jill?

It's the hottest day of the year so far. I can make out my mother from the subway exit two blocks away, dressed in white and spreading her arms at me and doing one of her dances. A heat haze makes her look wavy. Her hair is thick and black, her face expressive, olive-skinned, dramatic.

"Aren't you hot?" I ask when I reach her.

She hugs me. "It's so nice to see you, my darling! Look at you. Your hair! What did you do? Your teeth! They're so . . . great! Just great!" There is also pantomime, gesture, Japanese noh theater. She spins me around, looks, hugs again.

"Aren't you hot?" I repeat. The heat is making me dazed.

"I don't mind the heat." It's rising off the pavement in ripples. She hugs the van driver, who is visibly sweating from open pores on his reddened forehead, nose, and cheeks.

"Your mother is very nice lady," he says, in spite of the two hours' wait. I notice an accent. *Azerbaijan,* I guess to myself.

My mother and I walk up the stairs to her third-floor landing, and I think it's fortuitous that I've made it out to Long Island City on this hottest day of the year so Jill and my mother can have A/C. I'm not thinking of the inevitable swerve, though as my mother walks ahead of me on the steps I do think to ring Malaprop to beg for a reprieve. My mother can't actually be kicked out from the seven-day-a-week program. What would we do? It's unthinkable.

When she picks up, Malaprop starts right in where she left off, as if there has been no interruption of time or distance or mental distraction since our last chat. "It's more times than we realized, Elizabeth. The van company thought they could work directly with the client themselves, which I didn't know about, and now the normal procedure—"

Malaprop's voice drones on as I reach the inside of the apartment, my mother trailing behind, and walk into the bedroom to deposit the A/C supplies. There I am startled by the sight of Jill passed out on her bed.

Swerve.

I hang up on Malaprop. Just like that. *Click.* And she's gone.

Jill has cut marks and thin patches of dry blood on one arm. The blood is cracked and translucent, not copious, not like she slit her wrist or anything . . . *or anything.*

I call David, Jill's case manager at Bellevue, to tell him there's an emergency. I leave a message.

I don't think Jill's body is a corpse. I think, *She's not dead.* I think that I can see, barely, a small movement in her chest. Rather, I imagine what it would be like *if* she were a corpse. I am vaguely aware of my mother standing behind me peering at Jill over my shoulder. I see two images of Jill in parallax: one as she is, the other as a corpse. Slowly, slowly, the two images move closer together until they're lined up. Then I realize there's virtually no difference.

I experience the moving of adrenaline through me as a pulse. I walk to the bed. My mother is behind me mirroring each of my steps. Things could go either way. I put my hand on Jill's shoulder and rock her a little. My mind is also on Malaprop and the no-day-center problem, and the air conditioner and the supplies, which still dangle from my hand in their plastic bag. Wherever the swerve might be, I continue to believe in a small part of me that I have arrived at the apartment prepared for it. Also, I feel I am not really in the room but somewhere else, or maybe up in the corner.

Jill doesn't wake up, but she's breathing.

I shake harder and her eyes slit open.

"Do I need to call an ambulance?" I ask her.

"*Noooo,*" she moans. "I'm just tired. Really, really tired." She nods back out.

I wake her again. "What are the cuts?"

"I broke a glass in the sink while I was doing dishes. Leave me alone. You don't understand. You never understand."

"Understand what?"

She passes out again.

I wake her again. "You missed the van. They were buzzing and buzzing."

She pops up to sitting. "What time is it? Oh no!" Then she lies back down and is out again.

My mother stands beside me peering at Jill and then looking back to me while affecting empathic faces. She pantomimes concern, looks at Jill with the same mime expression, then makes an exaggerated *poor baby* pout, and addresses it to me, then to Jill, then to me. I try to reassure her by acting as if everything's under control.

My gesture may be empty too, but its effect is real, at least on me. I wonder if this would be different if I were alone. I wonder if I *am* alone. I didn't understand; Jill was right about that. My mother has been playing a role that looks like being present, and so I have been reading her as present. She gets right into her bed and pulls up her covers to below her chin and smiles at me and begins to watch me as if I am a TV, with an expression of amused curiosity and intrigue. From the bed parallel to hers, Jill blearily comes to consciousness and observes me too.

As if this is another of the most normal afternoons of the year, I work without thinking on the A/C installation with the foam strips and weatherproofing tape. The socket is ringed in soot, so I cover it with a sign and the blue tape—DO NOT TOUCH. Then I attach the power cord to a plug at the far end of the room and turn on the A/C. It is huge—14,000 btus—and I put it on 60 degrees and the highest fan setting.

This instantly blows the reset button on the new power strip. I set it again and lower the fan, and now it keeps running. It seems to do little to cool the room, but Jill and my mother are sleeping as if they're fine.

Looking back, I remember that there was a time lag between my perception of circumstances and my reaction. For that second, when Jill was lying there on the bed, she looked like she was dead. What would I have done? Now, I think, *Did I actually do this?*

I was operating according to *Hotel Rwanda* logic. You think you have hit bottom and then you're taken another notch lower, but you're still operating according to the idea that the old floor is your bottom. One death stuns you and then suddenly there is mass murder. I tell my students to watch *Hotel Rwanda* to learn structure. A swerve, I tell them, creates surprise and reversal and moves the plot.

The next morning, I wake up in my apartment to the new reality. I'd been trying to line up extra care to lessen Jill's afternoon hours. I was trying to solve the problem of not enough daytime care; now I must confront the reality that there's none. My new struggle is to recoup what we had.

David has returned my call and told me that he recommends that Jill admit herself to the psych unit at Bellevue, and Jill has texted to say she's going.

I should have been more compassionate. I call Jill and tell her that I agree with David and that she should go. We'll manage without her, of course, I say.

I make a list of people to call and one by one start leaving messages.

I'm still in bed. I make another list:

Don't make phone calls from bed.
Don't make them in hundred-degree heat walking down the sidewalk.
Don't give in to crisis thinking.

One crisis need not snowball to the next.
Every present moment exists in its own time.
The trauma of the present moment needn't infect the
  moment that follows.

Then I look up a saying that I read recently in a compendium of Buddhist aphorisms:

Do not encumber your mind with useless thoughts. What
good does it do to brood on the past or anticipate the
future?
  —*Dilgo Khyentse Rinpoche*

I make an appointment at a day center off Queens Boulevard where my mother could possibly start, though they don't take Medicaid, and walk to the Union Square subway feeling in control nonetheless. I am in my body, as if floating, lithe and in the air. *I will function, I will fly.* I think of the feeling in yoga yesterday. *I pulsed through the air.* The heat is already pressing down on me, and I think of what Frank said. *The air is meeting me.* The yogis are relentless brightsiders; Jill has always hated this about me.

On the subway out to the community center, I write more reminders-to-self in my notebook: *Be in the moment. Observe the flickering present. Hone perception. Act in the instant.* Another yoga teacher, Cyndi Lee, recently recommended subscribing to a daily cell phone widget from Swami Satchidananda. "They say really wise things," she said, "like, '*Don't worry. It doesn't actually help.*'" I add this wisdom to my list.

And then the train hits the elevated rail tracks above Queens Boulevard, and I move into cell phone reception and the phone rings, and I answer, and all my resolutions vanish. I depart the station on Queens Boulevard and For-tieth Street with the phone attached to my ear. I am wan-dering in the unmitigated heat and glare, lost on the hot pavement in Queens, just as forecasted. Since I don't know where I'm going and can't use the GPS on my phone while I'm taking a call, I sit on the sidewalk. Now I'm talking in hundred-degree heat on the pavement.

It is Sue, from the home-care agency that sent us Veta for twelve hours a week. We can barely afford Veta, but I've called Sue to ask for another Veta.

"It takes me minimum two weeks to do a search," Sue tells me.

"I really can't talk because we're in a crisis and I have to find someone right now."

"Let me just give you two numbers, two numbers"—and she gives me numbers for two emergency home-care agen-cies, which before hanging up on her I write down on a slip of paper that promptly flies through the air until I dash and catch it.

Before I put it away, my phone rings again. It is David. He says that he believes Jill's attempt to take her life "wasn't serious."

"She was attempting to take her life?" *I knew this, didn't I?* Swerve.

He and Jill want me to come to an 11 A.M. meeting at Bellevue.

"I can't. I can't take care of everybody."

"Yes, it's not an ideal world, and in an ideal world you could come."

I move in with my mother. There are no other options. I wish the circumstances had something to do with me, some failing—me, a child-woman, seeking the succor of a welcoming parent. I come to heal myself with maternal nurturing after a tough trial in the world out there, with a man, or a job—maybe drugs or an illness. Perhaps the world got too rough for me. The universe was unkind to me. There was never that out. My failing was being able. When everyone else falls down, I show up to catch them.

The hard part is the not sleeping. Starting at 5 A.M., my mother is walking around my bed in a semicircle talking to herself—"Who is she? What's she doing here?" I slide down my facemask, smile, say, "It's me, Lizzy, your daughter," and her face relaxes from fear to relief. "Oh, good. Phew," she says.

I get into a routine: when Veta comes, I bike across the river to my apartment to pick up clothes and go to a yoga class. On the bridge I feel the openness of river and sky. Life feels like life—*living*—not so much a problem as an adventure. I feel hyper-acute and present. I start to think of my days at my mother's as my job for now, and start to like it. Penn State employs me for nine months of the year, but stretches out my salary to cover twelve. I can do this for now, until August. I think I'm good at it, coming up with activities—art therapy, drawing in the park, speed-walking to burn off energy.

"The obstacle is the path," reads another aphorism in my Buddhist compendium. My mother is who she is. Giddy half the time, despondent the other. Chattering. She is full of life and a desire to communicate, a will to in spite of her lost language. I'm glad I can alleviate suffering by doing this job for her.

When I return to her apartment she's doing her old model's strut for Veta, striding along the length of the railroad flat as if it's a runway. Then she does a little dance. She is light on her feet, carrying her weight up high like a bird, dipping and twisting to create flamenco-like movements with her shawl. She's wiry, unstoppable. The long apartment is the perfect setting in which to vogue and act sassy.

Issues of placement: these prove the most difficult—more than the language problem, the excess energy in the middle of the night problem, the moments of panic—*Where's the other one* [Jill]? *Who are these people* [Veta and now a second aide]? More than these is this problem of things winding up in the place that seems wrong to me and right to her.

Jill kept saying I didn't get it. She was right, I start to believe. Life in Long Island City is chaos. I start to wonder if Jill's error was in thinking there was even something to *get*. But I also discern an implicit structure. Things are not random or chaotic, necessarily. There is a narrative.

Packing a bag for the park, I ask my mother to put the sketchbook and blanket into the tote. The tote and blanket wind up inside the sketchbook. When I wake up, the cat's litterbox is missing, or seems so to me. But no, it has been placed on top of the bureau, covered with first a layer of a plastic bag from the deli, then a layer of my shoes, then a layer of my mother's clothing, neatly folded. My shoes keep finding new homes: in the key basket, on my pillow. My pillow winds up on her bed. I come into the bedroom and both beds have been slept in. The cat, my mother believes, eats a diet of fruit and milk. I put out cat food and water at night, and in the mornings she replaces them with chopped banana, apple, and milk.

I think of Patañjali's *viparaya*. How many filters of knowing obscure my own experience? What makes my mother's less right than my own? What makes anyone's?

On the street, I hear a woman say to her children, "Move over so that they could get by." The wrong grammar sticks in my head—*wrong to me*. It's not wrong to the woman, who also speaks to her kids in Spanish and then Spanglish. In Spanish, you would say "so that he could get by" and it would be correct, because it's subjunctive. Many things are just a matter of perspective.

I have been exploring options for a place to move my mother when I go back to Penn State in August, and this seems to have exacerbated her confusions of placement. I show her pictures of my place in State College, where she might live with me, and now she thinks we already live there. This seems to make her happy. Perhaps the fantasy is as good as the real thing. If this is delusion—a form of *vikalpa*, perhaps—is it not also serving a purpose?

On a walk out on Vernon Boulevard by her apartment, she says, "Do you remember we used to live here?" It's as if all minutes exist in one moment.

"You know me, right?" she also asks.

"Yes. And you know me?"

"Yes. But I don't know how I'm going to get where I'm supposed to be." She says, also, "Wow—look at that! Look," but then comes back to this problem of not knowing, and how scary this is: "I used to be here, but I'm not anymore. I'd like to stay with you but I don't know where I'm supposed to go here."

"I'll take care of you."

"Thank you, honey, thank you very much." Then, approaching the apartment's outer vestibule, she tells me, "No, honey, we don't live here anymore, we moved."

There is a desperate panic to her angst. Her lostness has method, if to the unlost person it would be impossible to understand what that method is.

I think what's going on is that she's very upset about Jill's absence. "People could have told me!"

"We did." I have told her that Jill went on vacation, but I fear that the image of Jill lying inert on the bed has had a subliminal effect on my mother and that she now believes on some level that she witnessed Jill's death.

"I don't understand." She purses her lips as if she's spitting, like this smells bad, as if the not understanding is a mean trick on her.

Perhaps my mother's Alzheimer's-induced psychic despair is only an exaggerated expression of normal human angst. Is there a cure for existential grief? Slow down long enough to think about our deepest fears and there lies the human condition. Aren't we all unmoored, alone, unconvinced of our true purpose? There is no clear path to relief. Where should we be? Where should we be going? Do any of us know, really?

I've been lost. One time I went for a walk at a wooded writer's colony and couldn't find my way. I listened for the sound of traffic on a faraway country road, but when I located the source it was actually a stream. My path spiraled. I identified landmarks that looked vaguely but not exactly like ones I'd noticed minutes earlier. Even then— five years ago, two years before my mother's Alzheimer's diagnosis—I flashed to an image of my mother. She was always getting lost. I'd watched her solve her problems by trusting in fate and following an intuitive course. Fate and intuition were closely related in our family.

In the woods, then, I did the same. And I did find my way. My panic dissipated. My mother used to have this kind of trust in the universe, and so did I. But now I know it's possible to be irrevocably lost, untethered from divine protection and mystical intelligence. Everything has let my family down, even reason.

I have been practicing yoga because, at some level, I have been seeking yoga's essential goal: an experience of the present uncluttered by past or future. This is Samadhi, an enlightened and ecstatic state. That Samadhi is removed from reason and coherence is not, in the yoga texts, regarded as a hindrance. Now I must reconsider everything I thought I believed.

My mother's experience is one of disconnected, separate moments. Even up until a month ago I understood this in a positive light. Earlier, I even wrote about it in the *New York Times*, in an essay titled "Living in the Moment":

Yoga citta vritti nirodha—yoga is the cessation of the fluctuations of consciousness. This, from Patañjali's Yoga Sutras, was the first piece of a classical text I memorized when I trained to become a yoga teacher. Perhaps paradoxically, this also seemed to describe what had been happening to my mother. . . . Now I sometimes believe I am not so much losing my mother as communicating, more and more so exclusively, with that side of her that exists only in the present. . . . To exist outside of memory is to occupy the moment wholly.

Things look different today. The relentless and unforgiving present is a source of panic and terror. That moment is corrupted if it is a moment in perpetual pain.

In yoga class one day, Cyndi says, "Seek *nirodha*." She translates this word variously as *quiet, space, ease, lack of striving*. I think of it as emptiness. Also, I think of it as *cessation*, from that same sutra: yoga is the cessation of the fluctuations of consciousness, from B. K. S. Iyengar's translation. There are other translations: "Yoga is the restriction of the fluctuations of consciousness" (Georg Feuerstein); "Union, spiritual consciousness, is gained through control of the versatile psychic nature" (Charles Johnston); "The restraint of the modifications of the mind-stuff is Yoga" (Swami Satchidananda).

Each time Cyndi refers to quiet and ease I think, grimly, *Cessation, restriction, control, restraint.* I think of a present that contains neither future nor past—a moment so short as to be discontinuous with anything that came before or will come after. It makes me claustrophobic, this present— too fleeting to leave room for an identity of any kind. It is consciousness severed from context.

Three weeks later, Jill comes back from Bellevue saying she wants to move back in with our mother for good. It occurs to me that I need a vacation, so I make a plan. I will leave my mother in Jill's care in Long Island City and attend a three-day yoga workshop upstate, out of cell phone range. I build in an extra three days before the workshop on my own at the retreat center. I know this is very irresponsible of me. I seek survival.

It's a bucolic property in Delaware County, New York, with a private guesthouse run by a yoga teacher I know.

"No clocks, no TV, no schedule," reads her website. I arrange the daycare and home care for the week and beg Jill to troubleshoot on her own if there's an emergency. I will borrow a friend's pickup on Tuesday and cart in groceries, and then I'll do yoga and read until the teacher and students arrive on Friday. My plan is to drive back to the city on Sunday.

Midnight on the second night, there is a refreshing summer breeze pushing the curtains inside the window, and I am reading from a book of Buddhist proverbs that someone has left behind in my guest room:

It seems that often when problems arise, our outlook becomes narrow.
　—the fourteenth Dalai Lama

Instead of allowing ourselves to be led and trapped by our feelings, we should let them disappear as soon as they form, like letters drawn on water with a finger.
　—Dilgo Khyentse Rinpoche

Resourcefulness [means] that you can deal with whatever is available around you and not feel poverty stricken.
　—Chügyam Trungpa.

The present moment need not bring me terror, nor should any future moment. *Stay calm.*

The same wind propels the slightest wisp of a radio signal to my phone, and two startling messages appear. Of course, they are not surprising. I have no right to be taken off guard. One is a text from Jill:

Mm has disappeared. We were2 go2 fr appt and I left her
fast asleep while I ran out. I hid all her shoes.

And there is a phone message from an emergency room doctor at Elmhurst Hospital in Queens: "I'm calling regarding Michele McKee, who has come back to our facility after running into the street at some point today."

My world cracks into many pieces.

It's a mile to the nearest cell phone reception. The moon is bright and I climb to the hilltop without a flashlight. I reach the ER doctor. To him, I was just a phone number. He doesn't even know my name. He found my number because another ER doctor recognized our mother. When she got lost six months ago, police brought her to Elmhurst to check her vitals. Now she was back. Combing the records by date, the doctor located her chart. The only contact was my telephone—no name.

A doctor *recognized* her, in an ER in New York City.

The doctor suggests we move my mother from the ER to the hospital intake ward. There, he says, a social worker can get involved and help us locate a safe place for her.

As he and I are speaking, I see what is about to occur in a flash, in the instant before it actually happens. We've been rejected for Medicaid-funded home care four times now. I can't solve this problem. Just like that, this doctor will take control of her care, and suddenly our conversation will take place in an entirely different context from the version I'd felt stuck inside only days ago. I experience a grand sense of lightness and weight shed. On the other side of this conversation, I will have crossed a turning point beyond which I can never go back. I am no longer my mother's caretaker; nor is Jill.

He says she shouldn't move back home. I tell him that I agree.

I teach my students to write toward epiphany, and this is that. I am moving through a trial that will irrevocably change me. The world is slowly shifting, taking on a different hue.

I feel guilt, and also I feel triumph. And I feel awe. In her state of cognitive arrest, my mother breezed out her door and removed herself from a situation that was unsafe, unhealthy, and unsustainable. After all my hours of information gathering, and Jill's agonizing attempts to maintain her sanity while staying home with her, my mother simply flew out like a little bird and let the world take her into its embrace. "Just relax!" she used to say to us. "Don't worry!" Maybe she can take care of herself better than we can.

Jill is out in the world ten days exactly before looking back at her shadow and seeing the truth: this world is too rough for her. She sends me mood-swinging texts saying she will readmit herself to Bellevue, and then she does. Everyone's in the hospital now.

Within the week, I have given notice for the lease in Long Island City and found a room in assisted living at the beach for my mother. Jill cannot afford the apartment without our mother, and our mother can't afford it on top of assisted living. The facility is very peaceful, at the southern tip of Brooklyn. We can't afford it for long, but long enough to figure out something else.

I go to the hospital to accompany my mother on her move to the beach. I discover her wandering the hall by the nurses' station. She is ghostlike, dressed in pale blue hospital flannels and matching blue socks with white rubber dots on the soles for traction. She livens up when she sees me. She hugs me close: "Oh, thank god, thank god! Thank god, you're here. I lost all my money. My shoes. Take me home, honey."

The staff lets me try to reach the doctor from the telephone at the nurses' station, and I stand there for several minutes on hold while the EMTs and my mother get prepared to leave. As I wait, I reflect with irony that tomorrow is Jill's birthday. I was born exactly two years and two days after she was. I am on hold for five minutes, six. I look at the digital reader as it races through the seconds. The date reads 7/21. Then the timer reaches an identical count of 7:21 seconds. I note this distractedly. Then it hits 7:22—Jill's birthday. Then it hits 7:23, 7:24—my birthday. I stay on hold for another minute, two minutes. We're into August, now September. I see the whole year slipping by. What will come of the future?

But it is done. Jill left her cat Cookie with a friend before rechecking herself into Bellevue. The apartment needs only to be shut down. I have found a subletter to stay for the remaining weeks of the month, and he'll take residence on the afternoon of my birthday. Jill and my mother—they've moved out forever. I don't know where Jill will go when she leaves Bellevue, and neither does she. But it's done, here. On my birthday I will work on closing the apartment, the place where my mother lived as she slowly lost her mind.

When I arrive to her flat to do so, first thing, the new air conditioner shorts the power strip. It's the second-hottest July week on record ever; the *Washington Post* is calling this "Humigeddon." As soon as I reset the strip, it snaps off again. I set it once more and it flicks off a third time. The A/C runs its longest, for fifteen minutes, before it trips the breaker. I feel despair. I unplug the other items from the power cord and this enables the A/C to run for several minutes. Then it blows the circuit breaker in the basement.

The cause of the power overload is obvious:there are only two outlets in the apartment. One still has my DO NOT TOUCH note. Everything else—TV, radio, lights to three rooms—is connected to a single socket. There is an elaborate daisy chain of power strips and extension cords tenuously holding together everything. By the time I've disassembled the entire network, I've collected ten extraneous extension cords. *Ten.* This is a seven–hundred-square-foot apartment. A disordered mind put it together. Problems got fixed by adding to faulty infrastructures.

Another knot of cables lies between the desk—with the computer—and the file cabinet—with the telephone and answering machine. This is like a tight, knotted-up ball of yarn. I think of the knots and tangles that characterize the Alzheimer's brain—amyloid proteins, neurofibrillary tangles. The cords are like a map to the inside of a sufferer's head.

I thread cords out of tangles and loop plugs out of eyeholes. I think, *The beginning of the end is a long time away from the end.* I feel hopeless again. It sits in my gut, a dread feeling. In moments the grief lifts and I feel elation: *I am trapped . . . I will be free.*

I collect two garbage bags of clothes for the thrift store and three of garbage—mostly food I'd ordered for my mother and Jill, a hundred dollars in frozen pork and spinach. I carry the bags down and leave the garbage on the curb and the clothing in front of a thrift shop around the corner. Just Things, it's called: that's just right. The material world never mattered much to my mother. Once when I was living in California my mother had a piece of family furniture moved out for me, and the shippers lost—or stole—it. "It's just an object," she said.

Just Things is closed, but they'll find the bags in the morning, as if the stork dropped them.

Only after I head across the river on my bicycle do I remember that the weather forecast is for violent storms. Through three days of heat- wave the city has been storing up pressure. I'm back in the East Village sitting on my roof alone, having wine and looking at the sky and celebrating—or not celebrating—my birthday, when I flash back to the bags of clothing at Just Things. Friends had offered to take me out, but it didn't feel like a time to revel. Jill is still in Bellevue. My mother is at assisted living at the beach wondering what she's supposed to be doing and when I'll take her home. They are both homeless.

A dog barks from the apartment across the way—lonely, maybe? Where is the owner? How long has he been left alone? There are abandoned, lost creatures everywhere. Who will care for them? A different dog, higher pitched, communicates to the first one across the air. I hear the stray honk of a taxi and the nearing shush of car wheels rolling eastward along the pavement. I stare at roiling clouds in the sky and feel suddenly content. I am grieving, and yet to grieve is to be alive. The distress has turned to something else, an ethereal calm.

The mist has thickened my hair, and my skin feels moist. When the humidity hits 99 percent like this, I feel full and lush. There are the lights of the bridge. I want to eat this moment. My mother loves me. Did I ever doubt it? "It's like a drug," Veta had said, holding old pictures of us. "She talks to you and she calms right down. Pride and joy. Pride and joy."

Then the sky cracks and rain starts sheeting out of it. I think of those garbage bags of clothes at Just Things. Everything has gone to shit. Or maybe this is a cleansing. *Wash the rags in the cool water . . . Let it run down. . . .* Didn't someone write this into song one time?

The Wallet Lady

"Excuse me," a woman in the hallway calls to us. "Do you know where the manager is? I've left my wallet in my room and I'm locked out." She carries a sturdy pocketbook, which she holds open for us to show it is missing its wallet. She's dressed to go out—it's fall. *"Miss! Miss!"* she cries when the aide passes.

"You lost your wallet again?" The aide is from Saint Kitts.

"How will I go out?"

"Terrible." The aide tsks. "It's not in your purse now?"

The woman holds it open to her.

My mother lifts her shoulders in her SOL shrug and raises her eyes to me. "C'mon, honey." We pace to the end of the hall. "Where now?" she asks.

"How about down there?" I point to the other end of the hall.

"Yeah. Yeah. C'mon. Doopdy doo." She grabs me in an elbow lock and makes a dancer's kick with one leg for her first step, then the second. I join her. We're winded by the end of the hall. "That was fun. Again?"

"Again!"

At dinner, the missing-wallet lady sits with us. She leans forward and cups her mouth in a whisper. "I'm terribly sorry. This is awfully embarrassing. I've lost my wallet. All my credit cards. I'd meant to treat you."

My mother pats her pocketless genie pants and gives me an alarmed, private look. Her eyebrows meet in tips between her eyes. She checks the back of her chair. "Honey, do you have any . . . because . . . my purse. . . . Do you have keys?"

"It's on me," I tell the table, with a magnanimous grin.

My mother sighs in relief. "Thank god."

"You're very kind," says the wallet lady. "You're her sister?"

"Do you see that man over there." My mother gestures with a nod to a bald, hunched man at a table across the dining room, someone who lives here. She sees him every day. "It's like déjà vu, I've seen him somewhere before. I know that man." She squints her eyes, trying to remember.

"I'm her daughter," I tell the wallet lady.

"Daughter!"

The bald man starts shouting racial epithets in front of the all-Caribbean staff. "*Shvartzes!* Goddamned lazy. . . ." Every employee has stopped dead and now people are shouting, "*Enough of that!*" "*None of that!*" "*You stop that now!*" They look at each other and some of us and smile and hoot. "*You don't say that!*" "*Enough of that!*"

"My god, some people have not even a little bit of class," the wallet lady says.

"I've seen that man before," my mother repeats, staring at the racist. "Do you recognize him, honey?"

"Yes, he's always here. He lives here."

"*What?* No. I mean, it feels . . . misty. . . . I have a vague memory . . . like from a past life."

After dinner I sit on the other twin bed in her room and she strips off her clothes for no reason and asks when we're leaving.

"I'll have to go home pretty soon," I confess to her.

"You're taking me with you, right? You have the keys?" Her eyes are disoriented and angry and panicked. Also, she's topless. "Take me home."

"This is home. And you're not dressed."

"Then take me with you." She slips on a white tunic from the closet. "I have to go. We're leaving. Okay? C'mon, honey." She walks to the door and peeks out, then peers back with a conspiratorial expression. "C'mon, honey. Now. We have to go."

Moths

You come home from spring break and notice there are a lot of moths upstairs. You left the blinds closed in the bedroom, you think, so maybe that caused this proliferation of moths. Darkness. You open the shades, sleep with them open, which causes insomnia.

The next day there are more moths, and the next day more. You check all your sweaters hanging in the closet, but they're okay. You think of buying naphthalene. But that must be toxic, you think, so you Google "moth infestation" and also "non-toxic moth repellant."

Google tells you: where there are moths, there are sure to be larvae.

You think on this a few days, while killing a moth here and there. Moths linger up in the corner, near the ceiling, the next day more moths, the next day a dozen, the following day two dozen. Within a week you notice, during the day, that there are brown streaks across the top third of the wall, streaks of dead moth, a testament to your murder spree. Within a week there are moths everywhere, really, but the wool in the closet has survived. At night, sleeping, or trying to sleep, with the shades open, you lie awake thinking. You think, *Why are there so many moths? If there are larvae, where are they hiding?* You check the clothes closet, but this is not the epicenter. *Epicenter.* Google advises you to locate the epicenter.

One night, lying awake, you remember the closet in the other room where you store things. Rugs, a few winter coats. It's 5 A.M., and dawn is creeping in with an accusatory glare. It's a few days past the daylight savings change. The brightness of today's 5 A.M. takes you off guard. Spring always suggests there are things to be done, things to be accomplished. You've never liked spring, as if its optimism, that sense of opportunity, is something you can never match. Spring is the time of getting accepted to an Ivy League school or getting a job offer from an Ivy League school or getting a summer fellowship to study something at an Ivy League school, but none of that has ever worked out for you. You went to a state school, and you teach, now, at a state school, where you champion your students and tell them that they will persevere and succeed against odds. You feel anxiety about all those letters of recommendation you wrote in the fall. Are your students getting accepted? At your state school they have strict policies against grade inflation. This, you are thinking, in bed, at 5 A.M., is really not fair. These poor state-school students without the benefit of grade inflation are competing against Harvard kids with their grade inflation for spots in grad schools. Not fair, you think, while in the back of your mind you try to locate, mentally, the source of the moth infestation.

Your body seems to work ahead of your mind; it tiptoes to the other room, the room with the closet. Your finger flicks on the lamp, your eyes darting first to the ceiling, where your out-of-body-seeming self notices, lambent in the light, dozens of moths hanging from the ceiling by the sliver threads of filament legs. They are like miniature bats, really, and you wonder if you'll contract a disease from having killed so many of these moths with your bare fingers. You feel that creeping itchy feeling at your neck associated with pestilence and/or delusory parasitosis, something you've felt here or there in your life in the past when worried about bedbugs or mosquitoes or fleas, though none of these in the end escalated to full-blown mortal cases. But this case is real. You can see the moths and feel the chalky pulp of their remains between your thumb and index finger.

You open the closet and indeed find, flying in a swirl, dozens of minuscule moths inside. You see your green fall coat and shoo away moths from the collar. On the floor: your bags of knitting. *The knitting!*—ruined, you think, but you extract the shopping bags, shooing away moths, and discover that nothing has been eaten. You remove the yarn, skein by skein, salvaging each, killing dozens of moths by hand, gently laying the knitting needles to the side and fantasizing about skewering giant moths with said needles and wondering about the wisdom of the new change in airline policy you heard about on NPR stipulating that knitting needles are now acceptable to carry on.

The closet is very warm. A heat pipe runs through it. It's as if a steam is rising off the rugs on the floor, but this is just the whirr of moths floating in a haze of what looks like moth euphoria, moth delirium. You flip aside the rim of one rug and witness more moths, swarming, really. This is in fact the most repellent thing you've witnessed. The rug has runic larval patches carved out of its front, as if to echo its own Oriental pattern. These larval subtractions seem to be telling their own story. They *are* telling a story. You know the story, immediately.

The story is this: your mother died of Alzheimer's fifteen months ago. Plaques and tangles corroded her mind. This was her rug. The plaques ate at the fibers of her mind in the same runic patterns as on this rug. Her last words before she died were "That's nice." You were playing her a fugal Bach concerto on your iPod. *That's nice.* She seemed to relax, with the music, for several seconds, and then she screamed. Then she reposed with the satisfied alien grimace that had become the mask of her final days with the disease. Then she screamed again, but you were used to it. It didn't mean anything. The nurses knew this, too. The scream was just an expression, at attempt to connect to the world. She was the madwoman in the attic, your beautiful, once charming mother. *That's nice.* She still loved Bach.

Standing by the closet, at dawn, you put on a rain poncho. You heave the contaminated rug onto your back and then carry it outside and hurl it to the curb. Tomorrow is garbage day. You vacuum every corner of the room and put the vacuum bag out with the garbage too. The vacuum has inhaled hundreds of live moths, and they are squirming in the vacuum bag out on the curb. The problem is solved. It's done.

But, really, its mental residue is not gone. The next day you wake once again to springtime's 5 A.M. You think about *things,* such as: This house you own but really *owe,* to the bank. Those moths in the closet and the patterns their larvae formed in the old rug, the rug that you put down in the living room when you bought the house but that emitted this black sand that stuck to your thighs every time you sat on it, or if you turned it up at the corner there was this light dusting of it, a rug pad without the connective fiber—why did it never go away, though you vacuumed and vacuumed?—but the other day you discovered on Google that this was, actually, of course, larval excrement. You think about how, at age forty-seven, your age now, your mother received an inheritance from her father. Later, she fell into an obsessive rhythm, getting onto the internet, *clickclickclick*, buying things. Buying oriental rugs, Jill said. *Clickclick*. In retrospect, we thought she'd had Alzheimer's already. Later, when she really had it, she played computer solitaire on the monitor incessantly and drove Jill nuts. *Clickclick*. It's destroying her mind, Jill would say, but, perhaps, really, it was helping our mother preserve it. The carpet was one of the things she'd bought. *Can larvae cause Alzheimer's?* you wonder, seriously, and you Google it, but find nothing.

You hadn't noticed during the month you had the rug in the living room the little ruts drawn out by the larvae, the patterns like brain ruts going over and over the same old worries. When will my new book get sold? When will I get a better job? When will I be married with child with great salary with career with success with fame? When will I prove all my mistakes were for good measure, that I did them on purpose, that there was a trajectory to my life even if I wasn't completely in control? There will seem to have been an inevitability of retrospect, won't there?

During the day I see it, that path backwards making sense of my choices. I am a professor. My students call me

Professor Kadetsky. If I email my state-school kids wondering about a missed assignment, they email me right back, contrite, and show up in office hours the next day with crocodile faces. I glare at them. Water beads in their eyes. I say it's okay; they'll get a B. Life goes on. During the day everything, everything, makes sense.

Recovery

In the image of Jill in my head, she is fifteen. She twirls a Frisbee above her index finger in Stuy Park, and it is lunch hour. Her thick hair is buoyant; her expression is intent, powerful. She taps the Frisbee into the air with the point of her finger and then leaps up and spins, then lands and bounces the Frisbee on her index finger just as it descends from the sky. She catches it from under her leg.

Today she seems to not be making eye contact. She's found new clothing in free boxes near the methadone program at Stuyvesant Square, she's saying, and at Goodwill on East Twenty-third. She's really into patterns and fabrics now, and she's been carrying around two paisley shirts for me that she now gives me as a gift. They're beautiful, silk with appliqué. At fifty-one she looks stylish—she's wearing a tailored crepe teal blouse and blue slacks that match—and she is still strikingly good looking.

Where to start? The city-run Magnolia House women's shelter, near Broadway Junction in Brooklyn, where due to a bureaucratic delay there was no lock on her locker and all her meds were stolen—including the antidepressants—and Medicaid wouldn't replace them without a doctor's visit, and the doctor couldn't see her that day, and then her Medicaid was cut off and it took another two weeks to get the meds?

How many times have I intervened: gave her a lock just to try, and yes, they clipped it; contacted friends in Legal Services, pro bono lawyers, outreach groups for the homeless or indigent or physically ill or mentally ill. I've contacted them when her Medicaid has been cut off, when Department of Housing Services lost her file resulting in another three-month delay for her consideration for long-term housing.

Or the assault on her by another woman in her room at the Tillary Street Women's Shelter in downtown Brooklyn, a two-hundred-bed, city-funded shelter for women with "mental illness and co-morbid substance abuse disorders," according to its website—or, according to the crime-watch blog DNAinfo, a shelter "rife with violence." Jill asked to move to another room but was ignored, so she fled in fear of reprisal, spent that night on the A train and then the next awaiting intake at another shelter to get reassigned to someplace new.

The stories are all secondhand, the narration unreliable. There seem to be missing pieces. Was there a dispute over drugs? Did she score a Xanax to interact with her methadone for a heroin-like high, because it was all so stressful? That time she overslept on a Saturday and missed the window for her weekend-long supply of methadone, was the heroin really necessary to ward away withdrawal and a reprise of her chronic back pain?

She's spent more than four years now without a home of her own, though to be precise she didn't have a home of her own before she entered the shelters either. "What am I supposed to do, put her on the street?" our mother used to shout when I accused her of enabling Jill. For fourteen years, Jill had been relapsing and returning from detox, and our mother took her in. Denial and incipient Alzheimer's seemed to me, at the time, a potent combination.

I didn't know then what I know now—how once in the shelter system people get trapped there, especially when mental illness (depression) and addiction enter the mix. A person like my sister falls sway to a cocktail of depression, chronic pain, addiction recidivism, the flaws of methadone maintenance, roadblocks in the bureaucratic public services that often require daylong waits in line to recertify or win back eligibility.

It was my decision to move our mother, after all, robbing Jill of her spot, a twin bed across the bedroom from our mother, the two beds sticking out from the wall like piano keys, just like the beds when Jill and I shared a childhood bedroom. It was I who called the (duly elated) landlady to tell her I was terminating our mother's lease. It was I who contracted with the assisted living center in Sheepshead Bay to take in our mother. The costs would more than double our mother's habitual living expenses, plus rent. There was no money to keep the apartment anyway, but where would Jill go?

She doesn't tell me things unless I ask, and when I ask she seems to tell me the truth. Often I don't want to know. This attitude of hers, this give and take—*If you want to be invited into my misery I will let you in*—makes me feel complicit, and on the flip side it makes me feel that I need to fix things, that I need to do what I would do if I were to find myself in Jill's situation. I would game the system, call a higher up, stay up all night until I'd commandeered an elegant escape.

I am not Jill, but I, too, feel defeated, clamped in the vise of a dysfunctional society, trapped at the bottom of the social ladder, unable to break free. I can't control her. Perhaps *she* can't control her either, and she feels the same deadened depression I do when I contemplate this reality too deeply, this inability to change things, this lack of power over the very basic elements of survival and recovery.

"I can't fix it," I used to say to Jill: when Veta didn't show up one time; when our mother was leaving her keys in the oven, putting cookies in the cat bowl, defecating in the shower.

"What am I supposed to do?" Jill ranted. "I can't live like this."

"I can't fix it."

"Why don't you come live here? Why won't you stay over and take care of her?"

"Because you need your bed. Where would you go?"

Then I put everything into boxes and stored them in Pennsylvania: Jill's 1961 Gibson guitar on which she used to play Led Zeppelin's "Kashmir" note for note; the piano, which my mother paid off on her own after the divorce—it's in the divorce agreement—and that my mother eventually gave to Jill because it was Jill who could work herself into a fury playing the last movement of Beethoven's *Emperor Concerto.*

After a month at Bellevue, Jill moved to drug rehab in Poughkeepsie for another month, and from there got placed in a "three-quarter house" where people were smoking crack in the lobby, so she told me she might go back to rehab in Poughkeepsie. Then Superstorm Irene struck while I was in Pennsylvania teaching, and I didn't hear from Jill for another three weeks. I thought she might have died. Even our father got involved, calling me every day to ask if I'd heard from her. I combed her bank records, finding nothing but one ATM withdrawal in Westchester somewhere, and I called every rehab nearby trying to find her, but of course no one would tell me anything.

Then she called one afternoon from Brooklyn. "I told you I was going to rehab in Poughkeepsie."

"No, you didn't. You said you might go."

"I thought I told you I was going."

"I thought you were dead.

"I'm sorry."

During Irene, the assisted living center lost our mother. They relocated her from the facility at the beach to another facility operated by the same owners. There, in the unfamiliar setting, she apparently refused to stay in her area and shouted at the aides when they tried to direct her to her new space, so they sent her to a hospital, as they always did when a patient became impossible to control. The staff called me at ten at night in Pennsylvania to tell me about it. Our mother was at Maimonides Hospital in Brooklyn, they said, but when I called Maimonides she wasn't there. I called the assisted living center again and someone very exasperated said they were trying to keep track of a lot of people and it was the middle of the night. It took me two days to find out they'd actually meant Methodist.

After Poughkeepsie Jill got located to a homeless shelter in the old Armory building in Park Slope, which wasn't so bad in context, just down the street from all the $2 million brownstones.

That December our mother was back in Methodist Hospital after again failing to comply at the assisted living center. Then, sedated, she fell while being held by a nurse as she was getting into bed. She broke her hip. I approved an operation to repair it, and the doctor called me afterward in Pennsylvania and told me it had gone well. In retrospect I am sure this was a lie. My mother had an advance directive saying she did not want interventions. At the time I didn't realize that this was an intervention, and a pointless one. At this stage of Alzheimer's a person can't really learn to walk again.

My mother had daily rehab for two weeks; then Medicare cut off the physical therapy benefits because she wasn't improving. Her condition had degraded completely, and she was not able to relearn to walk. She was restrained in a chair, because otherwise she would get up and fall again, and she continually tried to press against the restraints.

I was midsemester at Penn State, but really I was on the phone during office hours arguing with Medicare and trying to find other funding for physical therapy and also looking for a place that wouldn't overmedicate her. I drove to New York after my classes were done for the week and sat with her by her chair, where an aide told me, "I just imagine her getting hydrotherapy and acupuncture. I see her in a pool with a harness. I really think there are some things that could help her."

And I thought, *Why are you telling me this?* I felt rage. I felt defeat. *I have failed to get her these things. I can't find them. I can't fund them.*

She was still recovering from the hip surgery when I got a phone call from the doctor saying she'd contracted pneumonia from inhaling food from her digestive tract. This, it turns out, is common among people with Alzheimer's. There were the advance directives saying not to resuscitate or use life support, and it was the right thing to let her go now. She wasn't really living. I called the shelter in Park Slope and convinced them to get a message to Jill. I was in New York already, for the holidays, and took a cab to Methodist, and Jill met me there. I felt like I was throwing up my esophagus, and then I started to feel that way all the time, or maybe I'd been feeling it for several months already. The feeling still comes back, hasn't completely left.

Jill was able to get a pass from the shelter to sit with our mother after curfew during the final ten days of her life. Jill was with her during her last breath, during the afternoon of the eleventh day, while I was taking a break in an espresso bar across the street with two friends. "The breath just stopped. She was breathing, and then it stopped," Jill kept saying. Jill got annoyed with the nurse in the hospital, the funeral service lady, said she couldn't deal with this bullshit, the way the nurse wanted the body removed in twelve hours—"The body! That bitch called our mother a body!"—the way the funeral lady was saccharine sweet.

Jill went to the shelter. A friend and I sat at the diner across the street with the funeral lady, and I arranged the cremation and memorial service. I ate a toasted corn muffin with butter like I used to in the diner near Stuy Park in high school.

Jill was in Park Slope for six months, then went into rehab for a month, and when she had the van from rehab bring her back to the shelter in Park Slope she'd lost her spot. It was eleven at night and there was a two-hour wait; then a van came and took all the women seeking beds to the next shelter down the list. This was the Tillary Street Women's

Shelter. Later she moved to the Magnolia House, the shelter without locks on the lockers, then to rehab again, and now she's in East New York, out past the Broadway Junction subway stop in Brooklyn, in the seventy-fifth precinct, where a woman was stabbed almost to death on the street this month, leaving a trail of blood where she was dragged. The precinct has the highest crime in New York City right now, though crime overall is down 80 percent since 1992.

"I've been taken off the DHS priority list indefinitely because I had three dirty urine tests in a row," Jill tells me now, in response to a question about the perennial wait-list to get a shelter referral for long-term housing. She has an expression of complicity and commiseration. *Can you believe what these assholes are doing to me?* the look says. Part of its subtext is also *Can you believe how badly I fucked up again?*

"Dirty with what?"

She looks at me with an impatient expression. "Xanax." She rolls her eyes, sort of at me, sort of at Xanax.

I know she uses Xanax. I manage her bank account, funding it with small biweekly transfers paid for by our father. She spends it on clothes at Goodwill and toiletries, ostensibly. If I want, I can go in and look at where she's been using ATMs. It's a several-step process. I get the code for the ATM off the digital record and then Google it, and occasionally I find it's at the drug market at Lexington and 125th Street. At other times the evidence stares me in the face. There is a purchase from the Pathmark on 125th for 65 cents and a large cash-back on the debit card.

I don't look often, anymore. I made myself stop checking. I couldn't control the results, and looking at them only upset me.

I used to encourage her to keep a notebook—*write it all down*. "People have no class," she said, regaling me with stories about her roommates. When she couldn't, or wouldn't, I took notes myself—for instance, about the time she was driven to Coney Island in a van and dropped off for an interview to secure a long-term housing slot along with four other shelter residents. They waited in a crowded waiting room all day and at the end were told they'd missed their appointment.

I have trouble going back to them, thinking about it all. I often can't remember key details because I don't want to. Was it Klonipin or Xanax she was buying on 125th Street, or something else. Benzos. One of them, or all of them?

Jill is talking to me about how she has a supportive counselor at the methadone program at Stuyvesant Square and how she and he have worked out a plan: she'll stay clean, completely clean, for four or five months, and reapply for housing then, and do as many urine tests as they want. They'll all come back clean because she'll be staying clean.

This living in the hypothetical. This wanting to be angry at something, someone, so they can fix it. Get Jill housing. Get her out of this spiral. Get her out of the shelters. I can't fix it. I want to believe it's someone else's fault, or there's some fault in the system. There isn't even a system, if you think about it. This isn't something that works properly as long as its gears are oiled and maintained. You fix something when it's broken. Broken suggests an aberration from normal, that there is a perfect out there in which people keep their own best interests in mind and act according to will and do their best. Nothing's broken here.

Meditations on Survival

When I was growing up, maybe because it was the 1970s in New York City, or maybe because one of my mother's exes had stormed into the apartment one night when I wasn't home and hit her, I had a recurring dream about a menacing stranger entering our apartment. It's either an odd instance of foreshadowing or merely the prescience of inevitability that, in real life, the dream eventually came to be. It was 2005. Unlike my mother, I did not know my attacker. He was masked, anonymous. And he did not enter my apartment, but the vestibule and lobby downstairs, in a small building on the Upper West Side of Manhattan just a mile from where I grew up.

Despite these differences, after the assault, the old nightmare recurred, with my attacker playing the role of the stranger with inscrutable motives. He appeared nightly, often chasing me with a knife through the endless hallways of our old high-rise, the Pavilion. It had three elevator banks, each with three different designated pathways—to the service corridors, to the tower floors, to the base floors. There was a mazelike terror to the dream, as if the masked man could find me no matter how deeply into the recesses of my imagination I hid myself.

During the assault, I entered a different kind of interior labyrinth. I blacked out, lost seconds. This loss still troubles me. Perhaps this is especially so because it happened again nine years later—this loss of instants. This was during the birth of my son, thus creating an uncomfortable parallel in my mind. A third parallel, the fact of my mother's seemingly lifelong absence of mind, makes this all particularly disturbing.

As for those lost seconds during childbirth, it's not that I think I can get that time back. Rather, I want to prove to myself that I can be 100 percent present for my son as I wasn't during the birth, that I will never disappear from him, or, more specifically, disappear from him in the ways that my mother disappeared from me. The gambit, that I can be the mother I never had, seems to require of me some greater semblance of healing than I have so far mustered.

This tale is already becoming tangled, nonsensical. Maybe it requires a timeline of events so far. In May 2005, I was assaulted in the lobby of a sublet where I was staying on the Upper West Side. The next day, I was scheduled to pick up my mother across the city after surgery for her sinuses. She believed that her sinuses were infecting her brain, and that was why she had headaches and couldn't think straight. An ENT had told her that in fact she had massive maxillary blockage. I'd always felt that my mother was not present.

When I entered the hospital room, my mother looked at me with horror. She was still dopey from anesthesia, but even she could not ignore my own swollen maxillary area or the bruises around it. "What happened?"

I felt exasperation, desperation. If I told her, would she even remember? I rested my head on her shoulder and sobbed. *How, sometimes, you want your mother.* I narrated the events of the night before, explaining, also, that I hadn't been to sleep, how I'd laid in my bed replaying the steps of the encounter, which, in all, lasted sixty seconds. *A man followed me into my vestibule; he punched me in the face as I turned in shock to look at him; I blacked out and fell; he came after me again as I came to on the ground; he ran away when I screamed full throttle.*

"What?" She stared at me, focusing on my mouth, as if my words weren't coming out in our shared language. My familiar rage resurfaced. Bad news never stuck with her. She'd willfully forgotten the name of a man I'd recently broken up with after five years. She was ignoring signs that Jill was abusing benzodiazepines.

"I was assaulted."

"I don't understand. Mugged?"

"No." I tried to soften my tone. "He was trying to kill me. He didn't take anything. Assaulted." *The time she left me in a hot car while she went to play tennis. The time she forgot to set the emergency brake and the Volvo rolled backwards down the hill with me in it. And, then, it was the seventies. She was a young mother. She was single. She needed to live her life.*

Two years later, in 2007, the story I knew from as long ago as my childhood got upended. A neurologist at NYU diagnosed my mother with beginning-stage Alzheimer's. The fact that she couldn't ever remember where I lived or the name of my boyfriend—well, she actually couldn't remember.

In December 2011, she died of complications related to Alzheimer's. Alexander—who is now two—came into the world two and a half years after my mother's death. I'm not sure I can say *I gave birth to him,* given the fact of my lack of being there, really.

I remember meditating while Samuel Barber's *Adagio for Strings* and Beethoven's *Emperor Concerto* played on a loop in the hospital room, and then the doctor telling me to start pushing, and then there was that blip. I was vaguely aware that my partner was chewing on almonds by the bagful. I was aware that the otherwise yoga-like doula was physically anxious; you could see her skin pulsing and vibrating with nerves. And then, there was a needle in my back, some tubes. I was wheeled into a sterile room and saw many bodies in puffy blue costumes, perhaps my partner's face inside one.

Soon, my baby left my body, and for that short period in which the doctors sliced into me and tugged and chatted among themselves about some restaurant nearby and its fabulous ravioli, I left my body too. The umbilical cord was cut, presumably. But where exactly did that cutting take place: in my body, or outside of it? This baby had been a piece of me, membranes and strings and fibers a massive rhizomic mesh of me and him, and yet suddenly, this was no longer the case. I wonder how many seconds I lost.

During the assault, I also lost time. I don't know how much—little enough to see both the initiation of the assailant's second punch—then there was the break—and then the follow-through, and then to register his instant of hesitation.

That I blacked out during the moment I almost died: I find this indescribably scary. When I think of it I feel raw, or like 10,000 ants are crawling over my skin. I instinctively shrink from the feeling and attempt distraction. I was told, by a trauma therapist, that I should sit with the feeling. When I do so it stays, doesn't really morph or lessen or become acceptable.

I still have that old nightmare, now eleven years past the attack. It is a reminder of its lingering effects—chronic insomnia, a stuttering pulse, a panic response. It is a reminder, also, of those old fears from my childhood, that feeling of being unsafe. And it is a reminder that my mother also lived as a woman in our cruel world. And it is a reminder, more plainly, of my mother, of the loss of her.

At my infant son's bimonthly and then monthly pediatrician appointments, I was handed a questionnaire polling my mental health. No one handed me a questionnaire after my assault. The fact that I underwent routine screening for postpartum depression but not for post-assault trauma suggests to me that certain traumas are perceived as more heroic than others.

Have you considered the possibility of killing yourself? Why, yes. I was only sleeping for four hours a night. And: this tiny life, and all those sirens outside, and the constant onslaught of stories delivered via the news or Facebook of children injured or dead or abused: the boy from Syria washed ashore in Greece; the baby whose grandmother forgot to attach the strap on the car seat and then rammed the car into a tree; the father sentenced to life in prison for leaving his child in a hot car with the windows rolled up; the father convicted of the same for his senseless rage at his daughter's dirty diaper; the Facebook acquaintance whose infant son was so squirmy after a bath he broke his arm, and was now taking morphine; the Facebook acquaintance whose baby jostled the bowl of boiling water for a steam inhale and sustained a burn, and said mother who was later called about it by Child Protective Services. The stupid dangerous criminal things people could do. My imagination worked on a loop, fleshing out each tale with the characters transposed to my life. So, yes.

But no one handed me a questionnaire when my sister and I shared caretaking for our mother. Caretaking for a mother with Alzheimer's or being the victim of an unexplained murderous assault somehow doesn't catch the attention of the mental health screeners.

Our caretaking, as it were, took place from approximately 2009 to 2011—when our mother was then sixty-nine and seventy and diagnosed with early and then moderate and then advanced-stage Alzheimer's.

After the first time our mother disappeared, Jill picked her up from Elmhurst Hospital and brought her home. Our mother then slept for twenty-four hours and awakened refreshed and ready for another sojourn. When I suggested she wait for one of us instead of going for a walk alone because she'd just gotten lost, she insisted, as if she were a toddler in the process of acquiring new skills and independence, "Oh, that was a long time ago."

The following day, Adult Protective Services called me. Thank goodness. I'd been trying to call them! The caller told me they'd received a report that there was a senior endangered. "Oh, yes, she is. Can you help, please?" The caller gave me the number for the Alzheimer's Association, which I was already in touch with. The Alzheimer's Association had arranged a Safe Return bracelet for our mother. They had offered referrals for daycare, nursing home care, caregiver support groups. What they did not do, as a matter of course, was locate funding for caregivers, or fund caregivers, or explain what to do when one had a full-time job and a parent who could not be left alone for one minute.

The second time our mother got lost, she knocked on the window of a police squad car in the middle of a July day on the street near her apartment, which brought her to Elmhurst Hospital again. She'd left her Safe Return bracelet dangling insouciantly from the hinge on her desk lamp. My mother could not remember her name, and she misplaced her age by a decade.

When earlier that summer Jill attempted suicide, no one handed her a questionnaire asking about her mental health.

The misperception that the survivor of gender violence is the less noble sufferer might stem from the studies on trauma and mass disaster by the sociologist Kai Erikson—about Hurricane Katrina, the atomic leak at Three Mile Island, the Exxon Valdez oil spill, genocide in Yugoslavia, and a mining accident in Buffalo Creek, West Virginia, in

1972. Communal trauma hits harder, is a central argument in Erikson's writings. Somehow, since that influential work, surviving a sexual or gender assault seems to get erased from the category of surviving mass disaster (whereas war does not), but is seen, rather, as suffering alone—for instance, in Ben Yagoda's literary history *Memoir,* in which the so-called *misery memoir* of illness or abuse stands for the problem of narcissism in much autobiography. Perhaps understandably, suffering is all the more cinematic when inflicted by an identifiable antihero such as the Pittston and Buffalo Creek Mining corporations, the antagonists in Erikson's study of the injustices served upon six hundred miners and their families that culminated in the Buffalo Creek catastrophe and described in his 1976 book *And Everything in Its Path.* The chronic and widespread nature of violence against women perhaps comes across as psychological, or even hidden.

After I was assaulted, there was a bruise on my cheek that inexplicably would not heal. The bruise: my shame was so public, right there for anyone to see. It was not hidden at all. Sometimes I wore makeup to cover the bruise, to make it—the bruise, my victimhood, my vulnerability— disappear. But it wore off quickly. Sometimes I willfully left the makeup off, to wear the evidence proudly, though I felt defeated by the end of these days. It's hard to imagine now from a position of relative sanity how fully that bruise and the story it told overtook my entire being. The assault, the mark on my face that recorded its history, was my whole story, my whole existence. The man had left a thumbprint on my face, and with this he marked me as his victim, a victim, anyone's victim. It was an invitation to every other abuser. If they wanted someone to subjugate and degrade, I was that person. I was a moving target. It's hard to explain the logic of this now, but I believed it fully.

Around that time, I moved to a new apartment downtown, convinced the man was stalking me, though there was no evidence. My new place was near Stuy Park, which runs along both sides of Second Avenue. If I was going down Second and it was dark, I had to run the entire length of the block. It wasn't that there was necessarily an assailant hiding there. It was just that *if* there were an assailant, he would pick me. He would be able to read in my body my fear and vulnerability, that I had been marked.

A month later, I still had the bruise. I also felt lightheaded and nauseous. "Ah," said a doctor in the emergency room. He spoke with a kind of detective's relish. The fact that I'd blacked out during the assault suggested I'd had a concussion and, based on my symptoms, still did. The bruise: the maxillary bone between my right eye and cheek was fractured, unbeknownst to me. "Did you hear a sound?" he asked. "A crack? Like a baseball bat?" I detected a triumphant lilt.

No, I told him, I hadn't.

Also around this time, I met a hypnotherapist at a yoga workshop. At a group meal afterwards, she sat across from me. I felt her looking into me, though you didn't have to look deeply to read the story of my face. I explained everything. Perhaps she was hypnotizing me just sitting there across from me at dinner. She had dark hair and looked and acted like Susan Sontag. "Disease is what speaks through the body, a language for dramatizing the mental: a form of self-expression," Sontag wrote in *Illness as Metaphor*. My bruise was speaking my interior thoughts.

"I can make it gone," the therapist said, staring into me. "Like it never happened. It never existed. Erased." She peered into me steadily some more. Her image seared in my own mind, her jeans, her thick leather belt, her ankle boots, her olive skin and black eyes. She looked like someone I'd be related to. Like my mother. But of course, as I thought that, I understood that this was how projection worked in therapy, and no doubt even more so in hypnotherapy.

Disappear. The bruise certainly would disappear, but would the internal scars? I didn't want to make it gone. As much as the abuser had wrenched my story from me, now there was a new story, his story and my story enmeshed, and it was still my story, one I wasn't ready to give up. I couldn't willingly lose more seconds than I'd lost already.

In a 1991 essay in *Anthropology Today*, "Rape as Social Murder," Cathy Winkler, an anthropologist and survivor of a horrific kidnapping and rape, writes, "Rapists attempt to socially, psychologically, mentally and sexually define their victims. Rapists want to socially exterminate us. . . . Their torture and terror are their efforts to brand us." I would like to know why violence against women is the furthest thing from fitting into the category of mass trauma as studied by Erikson.

Also, I'm sick of talking about the assault. I want to talk about healing from it—becoming whole again. But can I even say I survived? I'm only even using the word "survived" to avoid the word "victim." To be a victim is to cede one's agency. But then sometimes agency is taken. "Any discussion of survivorship is dangerously misleading if it gives the impression that the main question is what the prisoner can do," writes Bruno Bettelheim in his essay "Surviving," about his imprisonment by the Nazis in Dachau and Buchenwald. With the exception of "not more than a dozen or so" escapees over the history of the camps, he writes, everyone who survived the Nazi death camps did so because the Allied forces triumphed. "All others, including me, survived because the gestapo chose to set them free, and for no other reason."

In early 1987, I took a women's self-defense course while I was an undergraduate at the University of California at Santa Cruz. In the course, we weren't allowed to utter the word "victim." When I "survived" my assault in 2005, I specifically recalled self-defense techniques from the class, which, according to the cops afterwards, saved my life. One technique was to utter an impolite, guttural, loud scream from deep inside. The scream perhaps had the effect of startling the attacker, who no doubt saw his victim as weak and small. It also had a kind of alchemical effect of transmogrifying the person under attack into a creature, an animal roaring, one making itself large, astounding, feral.

And is *gave birth* even the term? I had an unplanned Caesarean. My agency seemed to depart then as well, in that caesura between laboring and my baby's entry into the world. I didn't *deliver* him—a doctor did.

About two years after my assault, I was riding the F train home from Brooklyn. I saw a pair of shoes exactly like my attacker's. I never saw my attacker's face. This could be the man. Same height. Same build.

It seemed to me a perfectly reasonable supposition at the time. The assailant hadn't been caught, the cops having dropped the case with the cavalier attitude that the guy would wind up in jail anyway. The police had, however, unearthed two preexisting cases that they thought were connected. One victim had been in the hospital for several weeks with broken ribs and other injuries. The victims were all thin, dark-haired women with connections to Columbia University, where I was teaching as an adjunct at the time. The assaults were joined by a lack of apparent motive other than to do the victim harm or possibly kill her, and the fact that the attacker got quickly scared away by screaming. The facts didn't rule out my possibly paranoid belief that the man had stalked me before the assault and was still stalking me now, in spite of the fact that I'd moved.

I ran to the next subway car and watched the man through the interior doors. He seemed oblivious to me, but that didn't mean he wasn't stalking me. The train pulled into a station. The exterior doors opened to let in passengers and then began closing, and I quickly pushed through onto the platform in the instant before they sealed shut. This was two stops early, so I walked the rest of the way. Where did I walk? Afterwards, I had no idea. The world around me receded as the image of the crime scene took over: the man's black-gloved hand, the sound of my water bottle rolling across the hexagonal tiles, my scream eerily coming as if from somewhere else.

My mother had always seemed disconnected—dissociated, even. I attributed it to her emotionally abusive and alcoholic mother. Looking back, we knew our mother had Alzheimer's even as we were ignoring signs: the long stare; the cigarette with an inch, two inches, of ash dangling off the edge precipitously perched to fall, to leave one of those signature round cigarette burns in and on our furniture, on our piano keys, on her fingertips.

When I disappeared, it was not an unfamiliar feeling. To disconnect was something I had sought out, through meditation and even attempts at depersonalized out-of-body approximations of bliss. Certainly I had modeled my mother.

My son now suffers terrible separation anxiety, specifically from me. I fear that on some level I am echoing my mother's demeanor of distance, and that my son perceives this, and that this is the source of his irrational fear that I will disappear if I sit one room away from him.

In 2007, when I felt instinctually (though it hadn't yet been labeled by the doctor) that I was losing my mother even more intractably than I'd thought, I sought therapy for the assault. What happened on the F train seemed uncomfortably similar to the absences I'd always observed in my mother. I was not worried about my memory per se so much as I was worried that my mother had, in some small way, degraded her own memory on purpose owing to an unresolved, psychological need to practice avoidance. After searching MedLine, I understood that my theory connecting trauma and Alzheimer's held little scientific weight, though depression was linked in one study to memory loss, and lifelong trauma was also shown to compromise the hippocampus.

Perhaps what led me to therapy was the fact I saw myself refusing to step onto the F train now, and that I knew my attacker could not, rationally speaking, be resident on the

F train, and that I also knew avoidance was the fourth marker of PTSD in *The Diagnostic and Statistical Manual of Mental Disorders* (DSM), and that the number of places and people and thoughts associated with the assault that I needed to keep away from was slowly growing so large that the life I could still carry out on the margins of my avoidance was becoming alarmingly circumscribed.

My first therapist was Peggy. She was an acolyte of Bessel van der Kolk and Francine Shapiro, advocates of mind-body techniques for trauma recovery. Shapiro devised a treatment for survivors of the 1994 Oklahoma City bombing called Eye Movement Desensitization and Reprocessing (EMDR), which works according to a particular function that its founder admits to not completely understanding but has something to do with manipulating one's vision (or hearing or other sensory input) to redirect pattern thinking.

EMDR became more popular during the first Iraq war, but, as Peggy said on the phone before our first appointment, anecdotally speaking, therapists lined up to train to treat war survivors, but the people who lined up in their offices were survivors of violence against women. Fear lives in the body, is the principle. "Trauma has nothing whatsoever to do with cognition," Van der Kolk has written. "It has to do with your body being reset to interpret the world as a dangerous place. . . . It's not something you can talk yourself out of."

Peggy, however, worked on the Upper West Side. When I came to see her I told her that, generally speaking, I no longer came to her neighborhood. Her office was just seven blocks down Riverside Drive from where the assault took place. I'd come once but probably wouldn't make it a second time.

She nodded sagely. "Do you think the assailant is always on that corner?"

"No, of course not."

"Avoiding the place has no function."

"I know."

My second therapist went by her initials, E. J. She was young and petite, with long flowing black hair parted down the middle and a penchant for silk blouses with Peter Pan collars. In her sweet voice, she instructed me to narrate the assault several times over, and then to myself, and to listen to a recording of myself telling the story. This, she said, would make it coherent, placing all the details in chronology, revisiting the most painful ones—*black-gloved hand opening door, black-gloved hand zooming into my field of vision, black-masked face and white slits of eyes deliberate, concentrating, assured*—over and over, so that the memory was no longer so scary I had to push it away. She was brutal, E. J.

The technique was called exposure. Its founder was the psychologist Edna Foa, whose Emotional Processing Theory, developed in the 1980s, posited that trauma sufferers develop maladaptive "emotion structures," or in other words overreact to threat. To revise these broken structures, they must desensitize themselves to "information that once evoked distressing symptoms." To do this, Foa has written, "the emotion structure must be activated" (that is, the fear response set off) and "information that is incompatible with the erroneous associations in the structure must be available and incorporated into it" (in other words, reality and fantasy are set side by side, in a real-life encounter). "The absence of the anticipated negative outcome provides corrective information," she posits. The brain encodes revised expectations about the workings of reality, "thereby altering the pathological emotion structure." Detractors of her technique, such as Van der Kolk, argue that exposure is merely desensitization, which is not the same as healing.

For the culminating treatment with E. J., I had to revisit the building on the Upper West Side where I was assaulted. I had to let myself experience fear without "tactics" or "techniques" to make it go away, such as deep breathing, she instructed me beforehand.

A neighbor let me in through the vestibule without so much as looking at me. I walked into the hex-tile lobby and looked at the mailboxes. I'd been checking the mail when the man appeared. I hadn't thought about this detail from the assault since. The lobby looked smaller than I remembered, as if it were a childhood memory where everything appears bigger because you, yourself, are smaller in childhood. Of course in this case, I hadn't been smaller. I went to the second-floor landing. I remembered how, after the assailant fled, I'd run up the steps, and walked out later and seen a trail of my blood spots.

As I stared, now, at this hallway that was both familiar and strange to me, my cell phone rang. I saw on the ID that it was Jill. What strange preference led me to visit that personal hell and not my present one? I picked up, chose to pick up. "You have to help." She was frantic. "She's putting all the shoes in the cat box. She's. . . ." It's not quite accurate to say the spell was broken. More accurately, the former spell remained unbroken.

I continue to push away the feeling. Writing the words above, I have a textbook fear response: my pulse speeds up; my chest gets tight; my eyes water. I look away. I feel suddenly depressed, though I have nothing to be depressed about. I love my son. I love my partner. I love my job. I love my students. Everything seems pointless. Looking away is what one is not allowed to do during the therapy, yet, still, eleven years later, I must. I'm sorry, I am going to go to the pool now and immerse myself in eighty-three-degree water.

On the night of my attack, I vividly recall the investigating detective saying to me inside my apartment, me bleeding from my face and mouth and nose, a throbbing behind my cheek, where I would later discover my face had been broken: "An animal like this, don't worry, he'll wind up in prison one way or another. He probably just got out of prison. Even if we don't find him, don't worry. That animal. He belongs in prison."

The next day, sure enough, my assault case was dropped, because there was a police shooting in the precinct. Thus, I am left with a question mark. What did my assailant want? Did he want what he accomplished, to break me, to instill me with irrational—*rational?*—fear every day for the rest of my life, to make me realize that no strong accomplished intelligent educated woman is stronger than a man six-foot-three-inches tall, weighing 230 pounds, with black gloves and a face mask? What did he want? Had someone—some ex, some political figure in Guatemala whom I'd outed with my investigative reporting in the 1990s—taken out a hit on me? That was what it felt like, a deliberate plan to break me.

The rogue history of the PTSD diagnosis can be charted through the successive editions of the DSM. Over time, the definition has bent to accommodate pressure from feminists. PTSD was listed in the first DSM, in 1952, as "gross stress reaction," then actually dropped from the edition released during the Vietnam War (DSM-II, in 1968) to downplay the effects of the politically fragile war. The condition reappeared in DSM-III, in 1980, under its current name. That edition also named as a related condition "rape trauma syndrome." At this time, in order to meet the diagnosis for PTSD, a traumatic event had to be "an event outside the range of human experience." But most types of violence against women were well within the range of normal. DSM-IV, released in 1994, revised that definition to include "commonplace" trauma such as domestic and other violence against women. I can't really say whether the effects of such institutional change are being felt yet, though anecdotally I feel the lack.

After she broke her hip in the hospital, my mother didn't recognize me. She did not seem to be a living being. Her body reflexively pressed against the restraints, as if without a brain to guide it. She shouted at no one, shouted out to nowhere, "*Mama!*"

I thought, *How strange, she never even liked her mother.* Is mother a person, or an idea, a feeling, a physical sensation of warmth, of freedom from panic? Is *mama* another word for not being lost?

Mama. My son's first word was *mai*—which meant "more," "bottle," "milk," "Mommy." Now it means "Mommy," or "me." "Mai do it," my son says, when he is insisting I do something for him or that he do it himself, which seem opposite but also collide into one thing. Him. And me. Mama, a word pre-

and post-consciousness. Was I screaming "mama" in my mind those two times I disappeared? Will I ever find out?

I have a painting in my home by my mother. It is beautiful and crazy, a multicolored evocation of planets with all kinds of Richard Nash–like notations denoting their astrological position on a certain day, I think (though I can't quite parse it, to be honest), arranged across a scaffolding of crossed diagonals. Today, Alexander holds it up. "Grand-maman!" he says triumphantly, having climbed up onto a high shelf where he is not supposed to climb and taken it down. I've told him that my mother made it, but now he merely takes it as a stand-in for the grandmother he never met.

Such confusions are common with him. He calls a pearl necklace that my grandmother gave me "Grandma." He used to confuse me for a picture of my mother, also on that shelf, when she was pregnant with Jill. Now he understands that she is my mother, not his. He is moving away from the ur-stage, when *mama* means everything. He is separating. Now is the time. Ghosts live with us. Things come full circle. We accept the existence of ghosts. Alexander recently decided there were ants in the corner of his bed. For a few nights he wouldn't sleep there. Then he began to insist, "I like the ants! Ants my friends." A million ants covering me. The feeling of blackness that would overtake me. Those ants must also recede, in their time.

A Room in the Memory Palace

In the dreams, I have a secret deal with our old doorman, an Irishman nicknamed Cappy. He is keeping our apartment in the Pavilion empty for us even though we no longer hold the lease or pay the rent. I can sneak in whenever I want, and while I'm at it use the luxury rooftop amenities that have been added since we moved out all those twenty years back. My mother can use the therapy pool for her broken hip.

Usually in the dreams, though, my mother is newly cured. A miracle drug has been invented for the reversal of Alzheimer's, and it is working. "Remember when we thought we were going to lose you?" I say in the dreams. "Remember when you were so sick you couldn't remember who I was? And now, look at this, you're ready to go back to your life!"

"Yes," she says, "isn't it wonderful?" She lifts her arms in her signature airborne pose from her modeling days, and flutters them as if she's been freed. Her luminous smile and high cheekbones glow with newly lustrous, alive skin.

My mother is haunting me. I'm okay with that. The bigger problem is how every morning I have to assimilate the reality of her death all over again. It is not the memory of my mother or even the grieving of her that I want to be done with, but my devastating sadness upon waking from the dreams. Will this never end?

At one time, the prospect of breaching the entry to our old building did not feel so occult. In about 2009, I woke from a recurrence of nearly the same dream and I thought, *Enough. I'm going back there.* In real life, I was living on East Twelfth Street off First Avenue, 3.2 miles down First from our old home on East Seventy-seventh. Why was I thinking like an exile? I could go back any time.

In that particular reoccurrence of the dream, our old junior one-bedroom behind the metal door emblazoned 1525 was free of tenants. We were squatting in 1525, living in fear of eviction. Our mother had the bedroom and Jill and I our old rooms behind dividers in the living room. We went about our days as adults—I going off to work, Jill staying home to cook for our mother and watch her.

Nostalgia is a paradox of irrecoverability, a desire for not only the place of one's past, but for its memories in real time, for their return to populate the present. It is, as Svetlana Boym writes, "a longing for a home that no longer exists or has never existed." The past, in Janet Malcolm's depiction, exists as if across a physical border. "The past is a country for which there are no visas," she writes. "You can only enter illegally."

The mind, though, equates past with place. Place acts as stand-in for that vanished, desired moment. It is a problem of misjudgment, that longing. Perhaps this is why my dream self keeps searching out that loophole, the illegal entry point. In the dreams, I am always breaking in and stealing back our lease according to one ruse or another.

After I woke from the dream that time in 2009, I called the Pavilion's management company. I got a rental agent named Larry, to whom I suggested with just a hint of larceny that I was a soon-to-be married future housewife looking for a place to raise her family. I told him that I hoped to see a junior one-bedroom at middle level, say, around floor fifteen, and then I embellished my story with details about my rich but absent fiancé and our plans to have kids. In reality, I didn't have a boyfriend, didn't have a job.

We made an appointment. I dug out a reporter's notebook and, as an afterthought, a diamond-and-pearl ring given to me by an old boyfriend, and I took the bus up First Avenue. Coincidentally, on the bus ride, at Twenty-ninth Street, I saw Jill crossing the street to enter her program at Bellevue. She was wearing a blue-and-white-striped tank top that I'd recently bought for her at Target using our mother's money. I tried to wave to her, and then I called her on her cell, but she didn't pick up. "You're wearing the top I got for you!" I whisper-shouted at the window. Seeing her from the moving bus, through the pane of glass, I felt the present slipping from me, slipping too quickly into the past. I felt as if I had lost Jill, lost my mother, already.

In his essay "Temporizing," André Aciman writes that the "temporizer . . . forfeits the present and he moves elsewhere in time. He moves from the present to the future, from the present to the past . . . he firms up the present by experiencing it from the future as a moment in the past."

I was temporizing, surely. Boym's "reflective nostalgic" is perhaps similar: "Reflective nostalgics," she writes, "see everywhere the imperfect, mirror images of home, and try to cohabit with doubles and ghosts."

Larry was near my age, short and round, and wore a Mets cap. He lived in the Pavilion, he said, and had grown up nearby. I allowed that I, too, had grown up nearby.

In the familiar lobby, we passed the doorman station and then an Asian fountain framed by a bucolic tapestry of a stream and mansion that had somehow never caught my notice when I'd lived there. The tapestry was made of needlework, and had the date 1964 sewn into the bottom. Also at the bottom were the words, preposterously, *Nearby Country Mansion And Pavilion Circa 1850*. The image's quaintness and Anglophilia struck me as charming, but I recalled with a visceral tug how these pretensions had repulsed me here when I'd been a teenager. I remembered how Cappy used to look us up and down imperiously and how he once told MacGraw to use the service entrance. How he once told a boyfriend of my mother's who was African American that we weren't there when we were and sent him away.

The convenience store in back, where the Holocaust couple had been ever-present fixtures behind the counter, had been redesigned so there was a large sandwich bar at the side now. "Tuna no pickles!" Larry shouted in a Jersey accent to the guy behind the counter. "Just a little bit of mayo. Ta-ma-tah."

"Da usual!" the grocer responded, in the same accent. Behind him, a young Asian man with an apron had tattoos on his arms from top to bottom.

"It's like a city," Larry said to me, salesman-like. In the laundry room there was the same bulletin board where I used to post my babysitting ads, now lined with notices for nannies, yoga classes, and African masks for sale. You *can* go home again, I thought. Larry and I took the elevator to the fifteenth floor of one of the wings. I would see an apartment on the same floor as where we'd lived, but situated around the side of the building and to the west. As on my family's old floor, mezuzahs adorned nearly half the doorframes. But unlike in the past, the doorknobs and peepholes seemed too low, like in *Alice in Wonderland*. When Larry gestured for me to push open the entry door, its weight seemed too light.

I felt I was in Jorge Luis Borges's Aleph, the whole world—present, future, and past—involuting into a tiny wormhole. Down below, a child shouted in the schoolyard of my old elementary school. I looked down at the schoolyard from the window, which offered a view nearly identical to our original one, if slightly skewed. The cries of a dozen other children amplified the sound. When I attended that school, boys got into fist fights outside almost daily, and then more boys circled them and shouted, "Fight! Fight!" The echo of children shouting from that schoolyard; the raw static of city air fifteen flights up; whirling wind inside canyons made from indentations in the building façade: I had only ever heard those sounds here, and now I was hearing them again.

I could come back, I thought.

The cheapest apartments were 2,000 dollars per month, Larry was saying. I was paying half that downtown. With a roommate, I could do it. Larry was saying there were 860 units total. For a second I was a child doing math in her head again, trying to tally the exact number of apartments in this vast city. All those minutes doing that math when I was a kid, it never occurred to me someone actually knew the number. The vacancy rate, Larry was saying, hovered near 1 percent. My math brain calculated. At any one time, there were 8.6 available apartments.

I said goodbye to Larry, mentioning that I'd discuss rental plans with my fiancé, and then I strolled through the adjacent park, John Jay, and gazed at the East River. Two thousand dollars was less than the combined rent of my apartment and my mother's. We could move back in, the three of us. In the park, women of many colors were pushing strollers and holding hands with children of not very many colors. This world was peaceful and secluded and problematic. Why did I want this world back? *You do not want this!* I shouted to myself.

In the eighteenth and nineteenth centuries, nostalgia— literally "longing" (from the Greek *algia*) for "home" (*nostos*)—was seen as an illness that afflicted, primarily, soldiers and sailors. The cure was believed to be a return home. In the early twentieth century, nostalgia came to describe the particular loneliness of the immigrant, in part because of a famous study in 1932 by the Norwegian psychiatrist Ørnulv Ødegård. "Emigration and insanity; a study of mental disease among the Norwegian born population of Minnesota" documented a disproportionate rate of psychosis among those immigrants. Sadly, though, repatriation did not cure the immigrants' longing; on the contrary, the psychiatrist observed high rates of psychosis upon the subjects' return home as well.

Nostalgia, however, is not universally equated with sadness. In a four-part study conducted in China using just over a thousand participants and published in the journal *Psychological Science* in 2008, researchers tested the idea that the Mandarin concept of nostalgia—*oihuai* ("sentimental longing for") *jiu* ("the past")—counteracts loneliness. Wrote the authors:

> *This research documents that nostalgia is a psychological resource that protects and fosters mental health. Nostalgia strengthens social connectedness and belongingness, partially ameliorating the harmful repercussions of loneliness. This research constitutes an initial step toward establishing nostalgia as a potent coping mechanism in situations of self-threat and social threat. The past, when appropriately harnessed, can strengthen psychological resistance to the vicissitudes of life.*

Perhaps there is an elegant middle pathway.

Now, sitting among stored boxes in my basement, my mind flashes to that time when Jill and my mother and the cat occupied the walkup in Long Island City and I visited the Pavilion to, unsuccessfully, expunge the dreams. Maybe we should have moved back when we had the chance. Or perhaps, alternatively, the dreams are providing me some balm against grief, are helping me to process and relive that difficult time in some alternate way. Strewn about in front of me are my mother's journals from those months—objects I'd packed up and avoided looking at after her move to assisted living. A sticky note, as if written to a future me, says, *Lizzy—see Mommies Journal.* I focus on passages from around the time of my trip to the Pavilion.

> *It's very scary to lose your own thoughts and not be sure of yourself, at least that is my feeling. I think I need to be with other crazy interesting people.*

How can I find them—they must be around—Poor Jill—she's so good—but I think it's taking too much from her—It would be much better for her if I'm doing stuff with other old age nuts I think—I need to find a club or something and just go—how can I find a nut club? Old nuts clubs.

Check what is available in our neighborhood.

I can't find my pocket telephone—I really don't like these things! Jill called me earlier, and said she would call right back—It's now after 2—I called her phone but didn't get her—tried to leave a message but didn't do it right! (on the regular phone). I can understand that these pocket phones are great for a lot of people—myself, I just don't like it—I suppose they are good for emergencies, but I don't really like walking down the street on the phone! They are probably very good for emergencies though.

I need to pull in my energy—the house needs to be put together again—I feel so useless—can't find things—feel stupid—scared—only thing that I can do is play god damned computer games.

Evidently my pocket telephone is not working—Jill is taking care of it.

I am thinking of checking the elder program in Sunnyside—I called for directions to get there today.

I am so tired. I had a bad thing outside—lost myself more than ever—I wanted to go see the Sunny Side Center to see how it was. . . . I freaked more than ever before and totally lost my mind!! I was very confused and couldn't figure out how to get to 40th Street—went back to the 70th sta-

tion finally and came home! I felt so stupid and lost and couldn't do anything about it. It's the worst I've been so far—lost and scared—I did know how to come back thank goodness. It was very scary and it's the stupidness I've never felt before.

Went to C-Town later (4:15)—and had no problems.

Reading this now, I do wish I'd gathered up my family and moved us to that safe and familiar refuge by the East River. I wish I'd acted and not just dreamed. Maybe my mother would still be alive today. Life, in Long Island City, had gotten too hard. Maybe if I'd done it I wouldn't have to keep dreaming about it now.

I brush past several more unsorted cartons. Of course maybe I have this wrong. Why am I so focused on just our New York years? What about all the other nostalgias? The boxes contain items from the whole span of my mother's life. From the time of my parents' marriage, there is a trove of photos, photo negatives, letters, and unconverted Super 8 home movies. After my parents' divorce, my mother removed all visual record of my father, but I know that at least the Super 8s must depict him—their cartons are labeled in his handwriting. Why have I been ignoring them?

Of the time until I was three, before my parents' divorce, I have just one memory: my father is standing before a red leather couch in an airy room with several doors, and the Beatles' "Michelle" is playing in the background. The *Rubber Soul* album cover, with its swirly orange letters, is propped against the sofa on the floor.

Soon, I have opened the storage containers and am sitting on the ground, their contents now also strewn in small piles around me. I quickly realize that I know too little of that time to even place my memory of the red leather sofa. I have no idea where it takes place. I can't match the image in my head to any of the several homes pictured. From post-marked letters, I piece together that between my mother's pregnancy with Jill and my parents' divorce six years later, they held a different address every year. During this time, my father was promoted several times as an advertising executive for Westinghouse Corporation, his place of work shifting from Boston to Chicago to New York and then back to Chicago again. The constant uprooting, my mother told me earlier, was partially the undoing of their marriage.

Perhaps to heal, I must merely uncover this hidden time period. I send off the home movies for digital conversion. There are ten reels—all labeled from just the two-year span before the divorce—promising about an hour of footage. Not too long afterwards, a DVD arrives.

The home movies show a version of my mother I barely knew. She is stunning, lifting her long and elegant hands from her lustrous dark hair and then out to the sides in that balletic port de bras of hers. She is seated in a purple Bertoia bird chair and wears a taffeta homemade minidress with yellow trim and magenta flowers that I remember was modeled on a Pucci. She is twenty-eight. It is 1968. The reels feature my third birthday party, Jill's fifth. Our father, who rarely emerges from behind the camera except to take jokey director's bows, will be on his own within the year—my mother's petition for divorce will be filed in June 1969, and the divorce made final in August.

It's easy to read portents into the images. The stylish and even blissful mood in the old home movie is false, perhaps like most home movies and their corollaries today on social media. My mother's gesture of lifting her long fingernails from her thick hair will within the decade become a nervous tic, in which she pulls so incessantly on the strands in that spot that she is left with a bald patch the size of a silver dollar—a professional liability in her modeling work. That the film is silent makes even more palpable the way my mother is physical, luscious, embodied. But there is no chemistry between my parents. Another couple mugs, cuddles, hugs, jokes. My father allows the camera to linger as it follows the curving upsweep of another woman's silver glitter stockings and then sweeps down again to catch her matching shoes. It is all very *Mad Men*. And in my mother's gaze toward the camera—at turns vampy and contemptuous—her anger is easy to read.

What am I looking for? I want things to make sense, want a narrative connecting that severed, unknown time to our later years in New York. The portents give me that.

Searching through the boxes, then, for more clues to help me place the red couch, I find a news item circa 1968 announcing the sale of a home owned by my parents in Briarcliff Manor, New York, with an address and a photo. I look up the address on Zillow, and, sure enough, there is a listing, and the listing includes interior shots. It is the home in the reel with the birthday parties. I notice an odd slate landing, between the kitchen and a light-filled studio. Examining the real estate photos, I see that the studio has exterior doors on opposite sides. This is the room, I realize, from my screen memory.

And there it is, then. I have my past back. The house is not for sale, but its existence on a real estate site suggests I could buy it someday—buy my past back, if not now, someday.

Using data from the boxes, I go on to create a list of the exact addresses for all six of the homes that my family inhabited between 1962 and 1969—the one in Westchester plus three in Boston and two in Chicago. Interior real estate photographs are available for all but the last, the home listed in my parents' 1969 divorce agreement. The most beautiful of the homes, a midcentury modern split level in Deerfield, Illinois, sold most recently for $1.6 million, a startling amount. My mother's last place of residence was a shabby one-bedroom apartment in a building with no elevator, stained carpeting, and that ancient electrical system in need of updating. It took me until my forties to secure a job that paid enough to send a child to daycare. Jill, while no longer homeless, lives in a subsidized "supportive housing" unit in Queens, a tidy walkup that she shares with a troubled roommate. Where did our wealth go?

What is it about real estate that reveals our deepest desires, our weakest impulses, the irrecoverability of our pasts. Writes Boym, "The object of longing, then, is not really a place called home, but [a] sense of intimacy with the world; it is not the past in general, but that imaginary moment when we had time and didn't know the temptation of nostalgia." She equates nostalgia with, more simply, a reconciling with the loss of innocence. Forcing past onto present never works. To force the dualities into a single image—home and abroad, past and present, dream and everyday life—is to "break the frame."

Vladimir Nabokov also evokes this concept in his essay "Portrait of My Uncle," about the author's inheritance of a noble property from his uncle and then his loss of it during the Russian Revolution. *Snap out of it,* the author seems to be telling his readers:

> *The following passage is not for the general reader, but for the particular idiot who, because he lost a fortune in some crash, thinks he understands me.*
>
> *My old (since 1917) quarrel with the Soviet dictatorship is wholly unrelated to any question of property. My contempt for the émigré who "hates the Reds" because they "stole" his money and land is complete. The nostalgia I have been cherishing all these years is a hypertrophied sense of lost childhood, not sorrow for lost banknotes.*

Patrimony is a construct. I should, like Nabokov, toss off the fantasy, forget about recapturing the setting and even affluence of my old life, my place in a racist Upper East Side high-rise where I always felt I didn't belong. That $1.6 million midcentury gem outside Chicago, is that really the life I want? And anyway, now, it's too late. My wish dreams are further than ever from potential reality.

On a trip to New York, I bring my three-year-old to the playground at John Jay Park in the shadow of the great white megalith that is the Pavilion. It's a strange kind of comfort I feel, allowing my mother time with her grandson from her stance floating up above. She is real again. The proposition that a person can be simultaneously alive and dead causes no cognitive dissonance for a young child. To him, she is still "Grandmaman." What would it be like if she'd never left our old apartment and I could bring him here to stay with her? What if she'd never left the world?

I am drifting off to sleep. I shake awake before I'm fully knocked out and realize that I have imagined her there with me, again. This time, it's the younger version of my mother—from the films. Perhaps in time I will only revel in my memories. Insatiable longing will fade. I will experience only pleasure.

I know the importance of memory. In one of my mother's notebooks, she writes from a dark time: Jill was disappearing, not returning phone calls, going missing for days. "It's too painful to lose Jill—my mother, my sister—gone in the brain and love," writes my mother. My mother follows with a list of fragmentary half thoughts: "Demeter/ Persephone—daughter in the underworld," reads one. My mother is referring to the myth of Persephone and the water of the river Lethe, the river of forgetfulness.

In the myth, Hades kidnaps Persephone, bringing her across Lethe and to the underworld. Persephone's mother, Demeter, wanders the earth searching for her daughter. Underground, Hades feeds Persephone the food and drink of the underworld, the food and drink of forgetting: water from the Lethe, and pomegranate seeds. The euphoric qualities of the foods cause Persephone to forget her past, and to lose her will to return home.

"O sister, mother, wife, / Sweet Lethe is my life. / I am never, never, never coming home!" writes Sylvia Plath in the poem "Amnesiac." Edna Saint Vincent Millay writes of Lethe: "Ah, drink again / This river that is the taker-away of pain / And the giver-back of beauty!" {~?~TN: PAGE \# "'Page: '#'"" Might need to be cut/altered for permissions purposes.}

Treasure your memories, people say. Treasure your memories, treasure your *memory*. I can give my mother that. At the end of the myth, Demeter turns the ground to ice and threatens to never let it thaw. Because the land must provide, Zeus negotiates a rescue for Persephone. Hades agrees to free his captive, but because Persephone ate the food and drink of the underworld, she must return to Hades in the underworld every year. During that time, she will forget again, and Demeter will, in turn, freeze the earth. In spring, Persephone will recover those memories of what was left behind. She will reacquire her longing for them—and she will return. But the deal is always contingent. We can never allow the forgetting to consume us.